CONQUERING
CHAOS

By Catelynn Lowell
and Tyler Baltierra

A POST HILL PRESS BOOK

ISBN (Paperback): 978-1-68261-312-2
ISBN (Hardcover): 978-1-61868-923-8
ISBN (eBook): 978-1-61868-924-5

Post Hill Press
posthillpress.com

Published in the United States of America

TABLE OF CONTENTS

INTRODUCTION

There are not enough words to describe the love we have for everyone who picked up this book. Whether you've watched us on MTV as we grew from terrified teenagers that were forced to grow up way too fast or you just happened upon this book while browsing the bookstore, we feel very humbled knowing that you have invested in our story.

This book was written for one reason: to inspire you. Maybe you relate to the struggles we have overcome and you'll walk away feeling empowered to change your life. Whatever your takeaway might be: The reason we wrote this book was for you. Plain and simple. That's why we didn't hold back when it came to sharing our happiest moments, like our love story, or our darker days, growing up in the shadow of violence and abuse.

There's a lot to be learned from our story. The whole story. It's easy to forget that there were sixteen years before the cameras started rolling. And those sixteen years were filled with highs and lows. One thing you'll learn about us is that we are very open and honest about the obstacles we have faced, many of which never made it on air but have shaped us into the people we are today.

And it wasn't luck that got us this far. From the day we found out Catelynn was pregnant with Carly, we knew we wanted a better life for her. That meant we needed to better ourselves. We also knew that placing Carly for adoption, while it was the right thing to do, would be a sacrifice harder than anything we have ever faced. What we didn't realize was that our decision would give us the determination to go after everything we wanted out of life.

Life before Carly meant being shuffled from trailer park to trailer park. For us it was normal to have to keep tabs on an intoxicated parent or have to deal with the cops. We were all too familiar with the way that drugs destroyed lives, leaving children to pick up the pieces. Sometimes our lives felt so unstable we weren't sure we would even make it through high school. It would have been easy to blow off our education, to continue the cycle of drug abuse and teen parenting, but because of Carly we knew we had to forge our own paths to get far away from where we started.

Of course, there were bumps along the way. Choosing adoption drove a wedge between the relationships we had with our parents. Their reactions to our decision broke our hearts and made placing Carly harder than we'd imagined. At the time we didn't realize that Catelynn's mom would take it personally that we wanted a different life for our daughter than the one she had chosen for her own kids, or that Tyler's dad would rage against placing Carly with adoptive parents who could give her a stable home despite his record of being in and out of jail throughout Tyler's life.

With our parents pleading for us to parent the baby we had to take a good look at our lives. Could we provide a secure and happy home for a child at sixteen without jobs, diplomas, or reliable parents of our own to help out? Not only that, but we also had to take into account the long history of abuse and addiction within our families, some of which went all the way back to our great-grandparents. We realized that because of this history, we grew up seeing exactly what we did not want our futures to look like, and we knew the cycle would never end if we decided to parent our daughter in the same environment. We did not want to end up like our parents, and we certainly didn't want that for Carly either. By choosing adoption we could be the first generation to put an end to the vicious cycle of abuse, addiction, and poverty.

Even with all the backlash that came with our decision, we stuck by it because we knew it was the right choice for everyone. By placing our daughter for adoption we gave her adoptive parents one of the greatest gifts you can give, and we gave Carly a chance at the life we always dreamed of. From the moment we watched her drive off with her adoptive parents, we knew we were going to do everything we could to become people that she would be proud of one day. That's how we went from teenage delinquents to hard-working young adults with big plans.

We traded in partying and getting into trouble for jobs, eventually becoming caregivers for kids and adults with special needs. We started to take school more seriously because we knew if we wanted to go places we had to buckle down, get our diplomas, and start making plans for college. At this point we were making something of our lives together, and nothing was going to get in our way. Not the effects of our childhoods, and not any obstacles in our relationship. But that doesn't mean those things didn't creep up on us, sometimes testing our bond.

We couldn't erase the fact that we had gone through an eight month separation early on in our relationship, or the lies and trust issues that came from it later. We couldn't erase the sexual abuse that Tyler suffered early on in his childhood and how it had continued to affect him throughout his life. And we couldn't erase our ties to the past and the dysfunctional world we'd come from, which was still full of friends and family we loved with all our hearts. We knew we needed to deal with these issues if we wanted to make it as a couple and be the kind of people Carly would look up to one day.

We had been lucky to have had very little conflict throughout our relationship when we were still "just kids," but after Carly we didn't feel like kids anymore. Our relationship took on a whole new meaning. At sixteen we felt like adults, which meant we were now in an adult relationship. Catelynn's history of lying and the pain that Tyler still harbored from our separation really began to chip away at our relationship's solid foundation. If we were going to make it we knew we needed to heal so we could continue taking control of our lives and empowering ourselves.

This isn't just a story about relationships, teen pregnancy, or even adoption. This is a story about breaking the cycle of dysfunction and learning how to overcome even the toughest obstacles that life throws your way. This is our story and we are grateful that you have chosen to read it.

Thank you. From the bottom of our hearts, thank you. Without the support of the people who have watched us grow since we were scared teenagers, we would never have become the people who are now writing this book. During all the challenges and sacrifices, we were able to lean on the love and encouragement of so many strangers who connected with our story and reached out to tell us what it meant to them. Not a day goes by when we aren't grateful for the time you've taken to get to know us and hear our story. For hearing us, for respecting us, and for reading this book, thank you, thank you, and thank you.

CHAPTER 1:

A VERY UNUSUAL LOVE STORY

If you know us from television, you know us as a couple. For the five years we've been appearing on MTV, from *16 & Pregnant* to *Teen Mom* and all the specials and spin-offs in between, it's always been "Tyler and Catelynn," "Catelynn and Tyler." A single unit, practically joined at the hip. But in real life...

Nope, just kidding. In this specific case, the real story isn't a whole lot different from the one you've seen: We've been a package deal for a long time, ever since we fell for each other at the unripe age of twelve. That's not to say we're not individuals — we definitely are! But in the years since we were childhood sweethearts, we've shared the most meaningful and difficult experiences of our lives. We've grown up together, and after all the ups and downs, we're still a team.

We know, we know. You probably didn't pick up this book because you wanted to hear two kids from reality TV brag about their perfect relationship for a hundred pages. We promise we're not going to do that to you. But this isn't just "Catelynn's Story" or "Tyler's Story." It's our story. And if we're going to open up about all the tragedy, triumph, mischief and mayhem of our journey, what better place to start than that fateful year in junior high?

Anything Can Happen on the First Day of School

Tyler:

Looking back on the first time I saw Catelynn is like watching a movie I know by heart. I remember every detail.

Picture the scene: A middle school hallway crowded with kids, most of them holding papers showing their class schedules and room numbers. It's the first day of seventh grade, and the energy is high — especially for me, a troublemaker from the trailer park who's been raising hell since daycare.

As I slide through the kids in the hall, I look at my schedule to see my last class before lunch is music. I think, sweet! Easy A. I walk in with my chains clanking behind me and grab a seat, scanning the room to see what kind of kids are in this class, looking for anyone that I knew.

Then it happens. I see her.

The whole room seems to go quiet as I lock eyes with a blonde bombshell. She only makes eye contact with me for a second, and then she turns away to talk to one of her friends, breaking the moment. But I can't stop staring at her. I feel like a creeper, but I don't even care. The girl is cute as hell, but in a tomboy way. She isn't wearing tons of makeup and she hasn't styled her bright blond hair. She has on a couple studded bracelets, flare jeans and skater shoes, and a shirt that says "I'm with the drummer." Her smile lights up the room and her eyes are beautiful piercing gray. Plus, she's got bigger tits than any other girl in the seventh grade.

Definitely my kind of chick. I think to myself, "I have to have her."

The class ends and lunch starts. I hurry and scan the crowd of kids by the doors to see if I can spot her, but I can't. Pushing through the suffocating crowd of kids, I finally spot her bright blonde hair disappearing around the corner of the hallway. I jog to catch up and then slow my roll as I turn the corner, playing it cool, and there she is again. She's just standing there, the coolest, prettiest rocker chick my seventh-grade eyes have ever landed on, and I feel like she's just waiting for me to walk up and grab her by the hips and tell her she's mine. There's no question in my mind: I have to make a move. So I take a deep breath and walk right up.

But just when I get close enough to say hi, she spots somebody and takes off running. Before I know it, the girl of my dreams is locking her arms around some guy, and they're making out hardcore by the lockers.

My heartbeat is now in my ears. I close my eyes and sigh. Of course a girl like that would already be taken.

Feeling like an idiot for the rest of the day, I finally meet up with my friend Ash after school for our usual ten-minute walk home. She hitches her backpack over her shoulder, pulls out two cigarettes and hands me one.

"Thanks dude," I say, my head still full of the rocker girl. "I'm dying." I shield the lighter for her and then stand against the wind to light my own. We walk and smoke, making sure to cuff our cigarettes just in case a cop drives by. In a small town like Marine City, police will stop an old lady for jaywalking if they're bored enough.

As usual, we head to Ashley's house and straight on into the garage, which was originally fixed up as a room for her older sister but later turned into Ashley's lair and our traditional hangout. The door is scribbled with graffiti of all sorts of stuff fourteen year olds aren't supposed to be into, from pot leaves to retro mushrooms. Ashley throws on some Bone Thugs N Harmony, one of our favorite groups, along with Sublime, Tech Nine, Eminem and a whole bunch of rock bands. I wonder what kind of music the beautiful blond bombshell chick from today listens to.

That's what I'm thinking while Ashley grabs a familiar box from under her bed and opens it to release the beautiful aroma of weed. We spark up the bud in her homemade pipe, and finally I start to let it all out.

"I saw the hottest chick today, dude," I say after coughing out a cloud of smoke. "She has the biggest tits in the seventh grade, long blonde hair, and a smile that don't stop."

"Really?" Ash takes the pipe. "What's her name?"

"I don't even know, actually," I say, gloomy about it. "I didn't even talk to her, I tried to find her after class, but she's got a boyfriend."

Ash laughs. "Who cares?"

I cough on the last hit. Ashley knows me too well. "I'll get her," I say. "Don't worry."

When You Know, You Know

Catelynn:

I'll let Tyler direct that movie, but I know it by heart, too. The usual craziness of seventh grade was especially crazy for Tyler and me, even before we met. Tyler, obviously, had his own reputation going on. He was a real smart-ass kid, and like all of our friends back then, his life was rough around the edges: A dad in jail, a single mom who'd worked hard to move them out of the trailer park, and he wasn't exactly known for being well behaved.

And I could relate to a lot of that. Tyler describes me back then as a blond bombshell with a big smile, but at the time, this "bombshell" was living in a shady trailer park. I wasn't the kind of person to cause trouble at school, but trouble was definitely something I was familiar with. I've got all the usual "trailer park kid" stories. My mom's trailer wasn't as bad as a lot of the others, though. It was a newer model with a nice open-concept living room, dining and kitchen area, and a hallway to the right that led to the bathrooms and bedrooms. My room was where I showed my personality. I painted my walls hot pink and splattered them with neon paint that looked awesome under my black light. My whole door was covered with stickers. My sister and I loved scribbling little messages and drawings on our doors, and there was always funny stuff written all over the place. After I got together with Tyler, you could find "I love Tyler Baltierra" written in Sharpie everywhere.

But really, the trailer park was not a good place to live. We never had good relationships with our neighbors, and there was always crazy drama going on between the people who lived there. Drunken fighting, drug feuds, nasty kids getting in your face, you name it. And our nice, spacious trailer had its own share of that crap. Believe me, we'll get to that later.

School was where I escaped that whole scene. My friends were all trailer park kids, too, but school was a more comfortable place for us to just relax and let down our guards. I was a real social butterfly back then, which unfortunately took priority over being a student. In my own easygoing way, I was pretty bad in school. I didn't get called the the principal's office all the time like some people, but I wasn't getting any passing grades, either.

Tyler spotted me before I spotted him, but I found out who he was pretty quick. We had a few classes together, and it wasn't long before we were hanging out with the same big group of kids. We weren't close, but we were familiar with each other and talked casually sometimes. Of course, I had no idea this kid had already made up his mind to get me!

The first I heard of it was from our friend Alexa, who quietly gave me the news one day when the usual group was gathered at school. In true junior high school girl fashion, she just came out of nowhere and said, "You know, Catelynn, Tyler really likes you."

"Oh, really?" What else do you say? I didn't see it coming, but Tyler must have known what was up: When I walked out of the classroom, I remember glancing over at him and he was giving her the darkest death glare I'd ever seen.

So from that point, I knew Tyler was interested in me. But I still had a boyfriend at the time. I didn't know how *serious* Tyler was about getting together with me until one night a few weeks later, when I had a party at my house. All of my friends were there, including my boyfriend. And Tyler was there, too.

I can't explain how, but I could just sense that whatever might happen between Tyler and me would be something serious. Maybe it was the way he was focused on me, or the look in his eyes whenever he glanced at me with this other guy. Whatever it was, I knew that Tyler had made up his mind to be my boyfriend, and I knew that if I encouraged him, it would be a done deal. I think that's why I told him he couldn't stay at my house after the party. That wasn't true at all. I had several guy friends over that night, and my mom was fine with all of us kids being there until whenever. But when Tyler asked if he could stay, I lied and said no. I wasn't even sure why I did that, at the time. It was weird.

Tyler:

I begged Cate to ask her mom to let me stay over that night. I definitely had plans. The whole reason I went to the party in the first place was to scope things out, and the first thing I noticed was that she totally wasn't into her boyfriend. Every time he tried to pull her down on the bed to make out with him, she'd get up and walk away. When I saw that, I knew I was in. And I knew she felt it, too. That's why she wouldn't let me stay! She was just nervous because she knew, deep down inside, that she wanted to be with me, too. She knew if I stayed we'd be together by the time the party was over. She just wasn't ready for it. But right after that party, she broke up with her boyfriend. I went for it.

There was no big production about it. All I did was walk up beside her and take her hand. Of course, that took some nerve. I was terrified. It was the scariest thing I'd ever done in my thirteen-year-old life. But I made up my mind that that was the way to do it: I was going to run up and grab her hand, and if she let go, well...I couldn't plan that far ahead. But I went for it.

Catelynn just held my hand back. We didn't even look at each other. That was just it. We just walked on ahead, holding hands, and we've been together ever since.

No Ordinary Middle School Romance

Catelynn:

I fell for Tyler because he was always making me laugh. Whether he was writing funny notes to me, cracking jokes in class, clowning around with his friends, he always brought this fun, positive energy to the room. I was a social kid, but I was pretty shy and reserved. I loved that he was funny and outgoing. It helped bring out bigger parts of my personality, too.

From the very beginning of our relationship, Tyler and I have had a strong bond. Not just as boyfriend and girlfriend, but as really good friends. No relationship is perfect, but even back then, we had a connection and concern for each other that was really different from what we saw in other couples around us.

People think junior high relationships are no big deal, and maybe they're usually not. A lot of our friends at the time were going through relationships one after the other, dating just to date. But Tyler and I weren't like that. When we got together, we didn't feel like messing around. Even at such a young age, we somehow brought out these grown-up, serious instincts in each other. Suddenly it was clear that we both wanted a long-lasting relationship, someone who would be there forever. Of course, we didn't know how to handle that kind of goal right away, and there was a time early on when we broke up for awhile and each dated someone else. But we got right back together, because we both wanted to be serious and we had what we wanted with each other.

Tyler:

We started the relationship with a promise to be honest and open. We each brought out something in each other: Cate mellowed me out, and I inspired her to be more outgoing. But we had to stumble around a little bit to find that balance. I've always had a strong personality and always speak my mind. Catelynn, on the other hand, is a natural people-pleaser and grew up doing anything to avoid conflict.

I didn't want to steamroll over her, and I didn't want her to hide her feelings and opinions from me. So I put my big mouth to use and told her, "Hey, if you don't like something, you have to tell me. Don't just agree with me to make me happy." God gave you a mouth for a reason!

Catelynn:

It was really hard for me to get used to Tyler's kind of honesty. I was not the kind of person who stood up to speak my mind whenever I wanted. Growing up in an unstable house, it was always my job to be a peacemaker and saying whatever I needed to say to make things go smoothly. The last thing I ever wanted to do was make waves, hurt feelings, or cause a fight.

For awhile, I tried the same thing with Tyler. Whenever we had a disagreement, I would always choose the path of least resistance and go along with what he said. To me, it wasn't even something I expected people to notice. It was just second nature to choose the path of least resistance. But one day, all of a sudden, Tyler came out and said, "Okay, this is annoying."

Tyler:

It wasn't an argument — we never really argued or fought, and it's still very rare — but it was definitely our first big talk. The problem was that I could tell she wasn't speaking her mind to me, and she was always holding in what she really wanted. For example, I'd suggest doing something that I knew she really wanted to do, and I'd ask her what she thought. And without fail, she'd never say, "Yes, I want to do that." She'd say, "Whatever you want to do." And if I said, "Okay, let's not do it," she'd agree with me, even though I *knew* she was disappointed! I couldn't understand it. When I asked what she wanted, it was because I wanted to know! Finally I just couldn't take it anymore, and I had to bring it up.

I said, "Listen, I'm not into this thing where you say 'yes' and agree to everything I say. I can't have you pretending you're okay with something when you're not. That doesn't make me happy. I don't want to be with someone who goes along with everything I say. I want a girl who has her own voice and is confident about it. You can't be afraid to disagree with me."

Cate's reaction was the funniest thing. She had a surprised look on her face, like the idea had never even occurred to her before. And when I was done she just shrugged and said, "Okay."

"Can you do that?" I asked her. "Can you actually say what you want so we're not just always going with what I want?"

"Well," she said. "Shit, yeah, I can do that."

Catelynn:

After that, my habits completely changed. It was like I was just waiting for someone to tell me it was okay to speak my mind. The thing was, no one ever really had. Not like that. I know it had a lot to do with my upbringing and home life: When I got together with Tyler, I'd already lived in ten different places, and I was used to living in unstable, unpredictable, emotional situations. So speaking my mind and sharing my feelings just wasn't at the top of my list of survival skills. It wasn't something that had gotten positive results in the past.

But to have someone tell me for the first time that he really wanted me to disagree with him sometimes, that he cared about my point of view, was a big deal for me. That was one big way that our relationship empowered me from the start. And once I got the hang of it, it was on! I was objecting to things left and right. And if Tyler ever acted surprised, I was quick to say, "Hey, you told me to!"

I know a lot of people struggle with this same thing. They try to hide certain thoughts or feelings because they're afraid of how their partner will react. But Tyler and I made communication a priority from the start, and when we had an issue, we worked it out like friends. We've always been good at talking to one another and figuring out what to do as a team.

Tyler:

It hasn't always been easy to figure each other out. Regardless of age, the first couple of years of any relationship are about getting to know how the other person works. How do they process their feelings? What stresses them out? What makes them feel safe? What parts of their personality or my personality are causing issues? What's the best way to stop our differences from coming between us? It's different for every couple.

Catelynn:

In our case, learning how to be honest with each other made our relationship strong. Since we weren't hiding how we really thought and felt, we were able to trust and know each other better. And that made us *want* to solve problems together. When you're open to the other person's unique point of view, you double your power to figure things out.

It was never about erasing the differences between us. Not at all. I'm more reserved and easygoing and he's more outgoing and loud, and we pull each other out of our comfort zones. I've taught him how to calm down and not get anxious or mad about the little things that he used to get mad about. And he's taught me how to get a little tougher about what I want. And when we're facing something difficult, we each bring a different perspective to every situation that the other person wouldn't naturally think about. That's what teamwork is all about.

Tyler:

We've both mutually benefited from what we taught each other. We started working on this stuff when we were just kids, really. We've been a team for a long time, and the bond we have together matured as we grew up. We're not perfect, and we've had some rough patches. But once we figured out how well we worked as a team, we tried to keep that going. Neither of us ever had any interest in being one of those couples who fight hardcore all the time. What's the point?

Catelynn:

We've never been a fighting couple. We're just not interested in making each other miserable like that. In the first years of the relationship, we didn't argue much at all. If we did, we were probably drunk and laughed about it later! Basically, when we had a problem, we talked it out. That was our rule, and it still is.

Since we've gotten older and started dealing with more adult stress and challenges, we've had some bickering here and there. But overall, we can remember maybe six fights we've gotten into. Most of them happened in the years after we'd placed our daughter Carly for adoption. Those were some overwhelming times, and we're human. But for the most part, and definitely for the important parts, we've been a team since day one. Not only are we proud of that, but we're thankful for it every day. Without each other, who knows how we would have come as far as we have?

Tyler:
Just imagine if I hadn't grabbed her hand.

Catelynn:
Yeah, just imagine if I hadn't let him!

Closing Thoughts

From the very beginning and continuing to this day, we get asked for relationship advice. Even our parents ask us! We try to give the best advice we can, but all we can really do is share what we've learned from our own experiences. Every single time, it boils down to a few important things.

First, be with the person you want to be with. Don't just date to date, or date because you're afraid to be alone. A good relationship is based on mutual love and dedication, and that's all there is to it.

Second, honesty is absolutely necessary in a relationship. Be open about your feelings and what you want, and make sure the other person feels safe doing the same thing with you. Don't let problems build up in silence because you're afraid to bring them up. That's like throwing a grenade under the rug. It *will* blow up later, and it'll cause a lot more destruction than if you would have just talked it out in the first place.

Third, be kind to each other. Never say or do things just to hurt the other person. If you're lucky enough to be with someone who trusts you enough to show you their weaknesses, the worst thing you can possibly do is turn around and use that against them. No low blows. Ever.

Fourth, respect the other person's point of view. Even if you don't agree with what they're saying, try to see where they're coming from. In the end you might have to agree to disagree, but at least you'll know you respected each other enough to try and understand why. And who knows? They might be seeing something important from their point of view that you just weren't able to see from yours.

These things are all easier said than done. Emotions can get in the way, and people make mistakes. That's why relationships are hard! But if you work together with love, honesty, kindness and respect, you can take on the world as a team. Like we always say, we can only speak from our own experience. But working on these good habits made our relationship a source of strength that got us through the most difficult experiences of our lives. In the years since we joined hands for the first time, we've had to draw on that strength many, many times. If we hadn't been able to turn to each other when times were dark, who knows where we would be now? Probably not writing this book!

CHAPTER 2:

" BAD KIDS "

Ever looked at a young person and saw something in them that made you say, "That's a good kid"? We've heard that said about us a few times in the years since we started sharing our lives in the public eye. "They're good kids." It makes us feel good to hear that, but it also makes us wonder sometimes: What does that mean, really, to be a "good kid"? People make it sound like it's something you either are or you aren't. Like there's some sign they can spot early on that says, "This kid is gonna grow up right." Sometimes they're right. And it's a nice thing for a kid to hear, that they're "good" — and it gives them pride, something to live up to.

But we wouldn't have that idea of "good kids" if we didn't have an idea of "bad kids" to compare it to. And for every kid in school who grows up hearing they're good, there's another one wearing the other label. You can probably think of one right now. Maybe you're a teacher and you've got a boy in your class who just has no respect for rules or authority. Maybe you remember a girl from seventh grade with a mean streak who was always picking on other kids. Maybe you're a parent with a teenager whose only goal in life seems to be to make your life miserable.

Or maybe you *were* a "bad kid." Like us.

Yep. That's right. People don't seem to take it seriously when we tell them, but it's true: We didn't start out as the "good kids" we might have come across as on TV. *Hell* no! Back in the day, we were more like the ones the "good kids" weren't allowed to hang out with. The fact is if you'd seen us before MTV, back in junior high or even in elementary school, your first thought probably wouldn't have been, "Those kids are definitely gonna turn out right." More likely you would have shaken your head. You might not have come right out and called us "bad kids," but that's what plenty of people thought we were.

We like to think we've proved them wrong.

See, it's never as simple as "good kids" and "bad kids." That kid in kindergarten tearing up all his notebooks and yelling at the teacher? He might be the most sensitive kid in class, if he could just figure out how to channel that energy. That first-grader with the sweet manners who always follows instructions? She might have problems at home that'll drive her to drugs by the time she's twenty. Kids are complicated. You can't just look at them and think you know what's going on inside, and you definitely can't say for sure how they're going to turn out.

We're glad people think we're good kids now. And we sure as hell don't want to change anybody's mind! But since we're lucky enough to have all these people listening to us with open minds, we want to show the rest of the story. We want to give you a chance to reconsider that whole idea of "good kids" and "bad kids," and how much people can change.

Daycare Delinquents and School Slackers

Tyler:

Trouble started early with me. I got kicked out of every daycare I was ever in. How, right? Well, I was very defiant toward any kind of authoritative figure. Even before I was five years old I remember thinking in my head, "What gives you the right to tell me what to do? Who gave you the title to tell me that I'm wrong because I don't agree with what you're saying? Just because you were born a few years before me?" I just wanted to battle them constantly: Cops, teachers, parents, anybody in charge.

The first time I remember really getting into it with a teacher was at a monastery daycare. It was run by nuns, and the place had a strict, crazy, cultish atmosphere. It wasn't the right place for me from the start, to put it bluntly. For example, when you got in trouble, the nuns used to put you in an extreme time-out. They'd lock you in this little room with the lights off, nothing but a filing cabinet and a chair facing the window, and they'd tell you to sit there quietly, think about what you did, and pray.

That wasn't working for me. As soon as I knew the door was locked, I started kicking it as hard as I could. I kicked it and kicked it and kicked it. Nuns are really patient, you know. They probably thought I'd wear myself out. So they let me kick my heart out...until the wood started cracking. Then it was on. When the nun opened the door, she was really upset, but I was in beast mode: I got a hold of that filing cabinet and shoved the whole thing over. Even worse, the corner of that thing nicked the nun's arm, and she freaked out. That was it for monastery daycare. It was like, "Take your crazy devil son and get the hell out of here!"

That last daycare, though, that worked out. It was the first one I didn't get kicked out of, which was good, since it was the last one left in the county. The woman in charge was named Debbie, and she worked a miracle on me. All she really did was take the time to talk to me, individually, instead of just making me part of the group. She never just treated kids as kids. She tried to understand them and communicate with them. When she told me to do something and I said "I don't wanna do that," she didn't just say "Well you have to." She said, "Well, why not? Why don't you wanna do that?"

That worked like magic. I did great at that daycare! I was there for about a year, right up until my mom saved up enough to buy a house and we packed up and moved forty miles away. The last day I was at daycare, that teacher was bawling her eyes out. When I left she told me, "I will never, ever, ever forget you. I will remember you for the rest of my life." I said the same thing to her, and it was true. I do still remember everything she did for me at that crazy time in my childhood. So Debbie, thank you.

I did fine when I felt like someone was actually hearing me. I just didn't like being told what to do without a civil conversation. And honestly, that was the theme that repeated over the course of my years at school. I didn't even make it through second grade before the trouble start up again. Some kid had knocked over my crayons and spilled them all over the floor, and I told him to pick them up. Of course he said no. So we started to fight about it, and when the teacher noticed, she said, "Tyler, pick your crayons up." Well, that wasn't fair. I wasn't the one who dropped them! So I refused, I got defiant, and bam. I was suspended.

The second time I got suspended ... well, we'll save that for another chapter. ·

Catelynn:

I didn't really have problems in school. Well, my grades sucked. I guess that's a pretty big problem. But as far as fighting with teachers, I didn't have the same experience as Tyler at all. I was a really laid back person at school. I didn't act up in class or make people mad. My problem was just being a social butterfly. All I really cared about at school was hanging out and talking with my friends. So it was fine for me.

My social life was important, because I didn't really like going home. There was just no stability. That was how I got away with failing everything all the way through middle school. My mom just wasn't involved. She wasn't going to meetings with the teachers to see what my issues were, or showing up to parent-teacher conferences. Nobody ever made a big deal out of it or tried to get me to straighten up my grades. Well, a few teachers tried to help me out, of course, but it didn't really matter. Seriously, I failed everything. Our middle school didn't kick anyone out for bad grades, so they just pushed me on through. I didn't start doing well until later, in high school. For the most part I just floated through school and focused on hanging out with my friends, because that was where I could relax and be myself.

Basically, school wasn't the battleground for me. Home was the battleground. At home it was all parties and drinking. My mom had a different boyfriend every few months, and people were always over at the house partying and playing music loud. All the time there were parties! I used to get out of bed at night and ask them to turn it down so I could get some sleep before I had to go to school. And there was tons of drinking. My mom was always drunk. The only time she was sober was in the two years after my little brother was born. When that time was up, she went right back to her old ways, passing out at the kitchen table with the kids running loose. I'd have to put pillows under her head and make sure she was okay, then take care of my brother and sister. It felt like I was on guard all the time. We moved around a lot, too, from house to house. It was just never stable at all.

My mom and I didn't fight a lot, though. We actually got along really well, at least right up until I got pregnant. But before that, we were good friends. It wasn't the healthiest relationship, though. She never pushed any rules or restrictions on me, and I pretty much got to do whatever I wanted. And growing up in a trailer park without supervision, you know, eventually I did end up finding lots of stuff to do that I shouldn't have been doing. Tyler's a witness!

Tyler:

At home, my mom was begging me all the time: "Tyler, just keep your mouth shut, for God's sake, and you wouldn't get in trouble! It's simple!" And I would have to say, "Mom, I'm sorry, I can't." I didn't have those authority problems with her, though. In our house, we'd get into it, but then we'd work things out. She debated things with me. She listened. She let me have the conversation. It wasn't like "I'm 30, you're 10, and this is what it is." It was, "Let's talk about this. What happened? What are you feeling? Why are you acting that way?" She gave me the opportunity every time to explain what was going through my head. I still got in trouble plenty of times, but at least I had a chance to feel like it was fair and we both got to tell our sides of the story. That's what I wanted. I just wanted someone to listen to me, and then I was ready to listen back.

But the school wasn't really up to my mom's methods. Teachers weren't so much about sitting down and communicating through every problem. So my mom used to get called every single day from the principal's office to come get her kid. She'd say "Sorry, I'm 40 minutes away at work." But when we both got home, she'd ask me what happened and I'd tell her.

Sometimes I was wrong and sometimes I wasn't, and sometimes my mom had to have it out with the principal, too. He used to ask her, "You really believe his side of the story?" And she said, "You know what? As his mother, I have no choice. I have to. If I don't listen to my son, what kind of parent would I be? What's gonna happen if something really bad happens and he doesn't tell me because he doesn't trust I'd listen?"

Mom was right. There was weird stuff going on sometimes. There were times when teachers were really out of line. There was a time a teacher was getting in my face and saying "What are you gonna do about it?" I shoved him against a locker. There was a time in the eighth grade when a teacher swung his car around in a parking lot and said to me, "You lookin' at my wife? Are you checkin' out my wife?" What the hell is that about? So of course we got into it, and then I got suspended! And when I told my mom about that, she called up every single teacher from every class and sat down and said, "What the hell is going on? I have this teacher doing this and this teacher doing that, what is going on here?"

Just because you're a teacher doesn't mean you're a good person. It doesn't even mean you should be teaching. And sometimes it's those kids who act up who become the target for a teacher's aggression and anger. Teachers are people too, honestly. I'm not trying to make them out to be monsters. They're human and they get stressed out and sometimes they don't act right. But a lot of times when they act wrong with the wrong kid, the kid ends up taking the blame. And all you see is the kid freaking out at the punishment, and you think the kid has a problem with authority. But in fact that kid might be fine with authority, as long as they get a little respect.

Fighting Up a Storm

Catelynn:

Everything I said about being laid-back at school wasn't really the case once school was out. Before and after school, I wasn't always very nice. This doesn't excuse it at all, but mean behavior was kind of business as usual where I grew up. There was always some kind of brawl going on in the trailer park. One neighbor would start some shit with another neighbor, and then the families and friends would get involved, and the next thing you knew it was Wrestlemania. And these were all-ages events! Kids learn early in those kinds of neighborhoods.

Here's an example. One day I'm hanging out at home in the trailer park with my mom and my aunt when we hear a bunch of commotion. My mom's boyfriend at the time is fighting with some other guy in the neighborhood, and they're kicking up a fuss out on the street. So we walk out to see what the hell's going on. At the same time as my mom, my aunt and I are walking down the road towards the fight, this crazy older lady comes screaming in on a bicycle. She spots us and assumes we're enemy soldiers. So she screeches up beside us, jumps off her bike, and wails *me* right in the face.

Of course that sets it off. My mom jumps on the old lady and gets her off of me, and they start fighting. So then I jump back in to help my mom, and we're wailing on this old lady together. Then the old lady's *son* comes charging in, picks me up, lifts me off the ground, and throws me through the air. I remember landing on my elbow, getting up, and running over to jump right back in again. That happened about four times, this guy throwing me across the trailer park road.

Trailer park beefs were a regular occasion. In fact, that one was a rematch. The first time my mom's boyfriend had fought with that guy, the dude had whaled on him with a tire iron. So there would be these long feuds and revenge sagas between the trailer park families, and I would always get involved when my family was involved. My main goal was always to keep the peace, but when a fight started up, I wound up in the middle of it. If someone came at my mom, it was on.

This stuff was constant. I remember once when my mom was having a party. My uncle was there, and my aunt, and a few other people. A car pulled up outside, and they all went outside for some reason. And a huge fight broke out in my front yard. Someone threw this handicapped man out of the car and left him laying on the road! When I saw that out the window, I walked out onto the battlefield to try and help this guy back into the car. I remember my uncle helping me get him back in.

Those are just a few of the battles I remember. It was chaos all the time. I didn't like it, and I didn't thrive on it, but I was familiar with it. It was normal to me.

Tyler:

I got into it with teachers a couple of times. When I was in fifth grade, there was one teacher I drove totally over the edge. I punched a filing cabinet, and he stomped up behind me, grabbed my backpack, and threw me across the room. Then he screamed at the whole class to leave the room. I couldn't show my fear, but to be honest, I was pretty freaked out. I'd never pushed a teacher that far before. But when he got the kids cleared out, he turned and faced me and he had tears coming down his cheeks. He said to me, "Tyler, I want you to know that what I just did was not right, and I am so sorry." He told me he'd had his own problems with his temper, and he'd lost control.

I was like, "Psh, yeah, whatever." But while I was walking home, I started crying! I was so worked up with adrenaline and caught off guard, I sort of fell apart. Of course when I told my mom what had happened, she freaked out. She was about to call the school and get this guy fired. But I said, "Mom, no. He doesn't deserve to be fired. I was pushing his buttons and he lost his cool. Don't do anything." That put her in an impossible position, pretty much. But I said, "Mom, if you get this teacher fired, I'll never forgive you." She finally agreed.

On Monday when I went into that teacher's class, he had probably had a hell of a weekend. I'm sure he thought it was all over for him, but apparently he did a lot of thinking between Friday and Monday about how to make things right with me personally. I think what he realized was that I needed some way to channel all that restless energy I was putting into being a dick. I was always trying to be the class clown, always interrupting, always acting crazy. So that Monday he pulled me aside and said, "All right, Tyler, from now on, the first ten minutes of class is gonna be Tyler time. Whatever it is you need to get out of your system, just go ahead and do it. Then we'll have our class." And after that, it was like magic. The kids loved it, and I loved it. Every morning I got to have my Jim Carrey stand-up time. I got my outlet, he got his class back, and I ended fifth grade on the honor roll. Ten minutes of Tyler-time a day was all it took.

That experience hit me hard. This teacher who snapped and lost his temper ended up being one of the best things that ever happened to me. At the very least, it taught me that not every authority figure who scolded me was out to destroy my life.

Fast Times at Junior High

Catelynn:

By the time I was in middle school, I had learned how to act tough in certain situations. Most of the time I was the most easygoing person in the world. But certain conflicts triggered something more angry and aggressive in me, and sometimes things got violent. Like the time I busted down a door to beat this one girl's ass. No, I'm not proud of it.

It was the summer after the sixth grade, and I'd just gotten broken up with by this kid named Nick. I didn't know why he did it at first, but one day on the bus he told me it was because of my friend Katy. It turned out he'd dumped me out of the blue because of something she told him.

When we all got off the bus, Katy was walking ahead of me toward the trailer park where we both lived. I ran after her and called her out. This girl was about six feet tall, and I was just a little thing, but I was livid! I was yelling at her, "We're supposed to be friends! What are you doing talking behind my back?" And then right there, in the middle of the trailer park, I just went at her. I started whaling on her in the middle of the street with all our friends looking on. And when she started running toward her house, I took off right behind her. I whomped on her a few more times before she got inside and locked the door, and then I started kicking it down. I was just going crazy. But the neighbor next door started screaming she was going to call the cops, so I had to get out of there.

I went straight home and started calling people up to tell them this "cool story" about how "I just whooped Katy's ass," thinking I was a rebel. I was bragging away, thinking it was all fun and games and drama, but then the next thing I knew, I looked out the window and saw a sheriff's car pulling up. Talking tough to the sheriff didn't help me at all, and I wound up having to go to juvenile court. I was put on probation for ninety days.

Tyler:

Seventh grade, the year we got together, was was when I started growing my hair out, going to Hot Topic, wearing the chains and goth stuff, listening to metal and all of that. Seventh grade was one of the worst years ever for getting into trouble. From seventh grade on, I never saw the last month of school. They used to rush me out early. I had so many suspensions and stuff racked up that as soon as the teachers could, they'd say, "Tyler, clean up your locker and get out of here." I'd go grab all my papers and run down the hallways throwing my papers everywhere screaming, "Fuck you, fuck you, fuck you!"

Catelynn:

Tyler really was in trouble a lot in the seventh grade. I used to walk by the room where they had detention and always see him sitting in there. I'd poke my head in and go, "Tyler, what did you *do?*" And he'd say something about teachers, you know, whatever. Then I'd tell him what everyone else was always trying to tell him, which was "Tyler, keep your mouth shut!" It didn't work, but I tried!

Obviously I was getting in trouble, too. We both were in our own ways, but we didn't really do it together. Right around the time we started dating, Tyler had just started to steal a lot. He stole a lot of lip gloss for me, and I didn't exactly talk him out of it. It was kind of a Bonnie and Clyde situation.

Tyler:

The stealing became a real problem, almost like a compulsion. If I walked out of a store without stealing something, I'd get this anxious feeling, like, "Crap! Why didn't I grab something?" And it wasn't just lip gloss for Catelynn I was stealing, either.

Taking It to the Limit

Tyler:

At thirteen I was in the prime stage of my gothic appearance and bad attitude. My dad had just gotten out of prison a couple of weeks before, the first time he had been out since I was eight years old. He had just moved in with this desperate woman who, for some odd reason, thought he had the potential to be a stable lifelong partner. I don't know how she came to that conclusion, but my dad was always the best con artist. He could sell glasses to a blind man, and he was especially good at convincing people he was reliable and then using that to get what he needed.

I decided to stay with my dad for a couple weeks that summer. He lived in Warren, Michigan, a real ghetto cookie cutter of a town desperately holding onto the hope it could be something nice one day. My cousin Brandon was staying not too far from where my dad was, and we had plans to hang out and get into trouble just like we had the first time my dad had gotten out of prison. Back then, at the age of eight, Brandon and I had gotten our first tastes of weed, cigarettes, and beer. Now I was thirteen, and we were all geared up for another round of delinquent fun. For a couple of days we went to work with my dad, helping him install fences for some spending money. Afterward we'd hang around smoking cigarettes and drinking forties.

Then one night we got an extreme idea. The houses in Warren were so close together that most people parked on the street to save room in the driveway. Brandon and I decided these parked cars would be a great place to look for some spare change. It started like a fun game, crouching, ducking and whispering between the cars like spies. But then we slipped into a car and saw a set of keys in the center console.

We sat there and looked at each other in silence, and then Brandon started the car and took off. We went slow at first, on edge and almost shaking with adrenaline. But then we got cocky and started peeling out, screeching the tires and letting every whip and turn around a corner carry us into a whirlwind of excitement. After we put the car back where we found it, we weren't interested in looking for quarters and nickels anymore. We went hunting for keys.

We ended up stealing about a dozen cars that night. We actually couldn't believe how many people were naïve enough to leave their keys in the car in that kind of town! For the rest of the night we jumped concrete driveways, e-braked every turn, and skidded along curbs, blasting Tupac, Biggie, and Bone Thugs until sunrise. Finally Brandon dropped me off at my dad's girlfriend's house, where I sneaked in and slid onto the couch with adrenaline still flowing. That was a night I will never forget.

In those days I had a friend who would slip into houses with me, too. It was an adrenaline addiction kind of thing, like playing Mission Impossible. There was one guy we knew of, for instance, who mowed his lawn every week like clockwork. And I timed how long it took him to take his lawnmower from one end of the house to the other. It took exactly two and a half-minutes to do this one strip. So I knew I had two and a half minutes to go through the bushes, run into his house, get to his wallet, pull out some cash, and run out. I did it all the time. I'd take twenty bucks a time, and he had no idea. Or at least, I never got caught.

Another neighbor down the street was a target of mine, too. That was the craziest thing I ever did. This woman was typing on her computer in the office about fifteen feet from the kitchen. I sneaked in through the garage and went into the kitchen, where she had her wallet on the kitchen counter, and I grabbed it and ran. But I remember feeling so bad. I just wanted some cash, but I had this wallet with all her debit cards and her driver's license and everything. So I did something even dumber: I went back to the scene of the crime that night, crept in the same way, sneaked into the kitchen, and slid the wallet back onto the counter.

When I was younger doing all those things, I think I was sort of daring someone to catch me. Part of the whole rush was thinking I was going to get caught, but then I kept on doing it. It's like I was asking for it. I don't know. Maybe I wanted somebody to get me in line.

Catelynn:
Oh my gosh. We sound completely insane.

Closing Thoughts

You know, when we put all these stories in writing, we started to wonder if it was really such a good idea. We were worried we sounded like we were really crazy, messed up people. Like we said in the beginning, we get a lot of positive comments from people who have watched our lives and really feel like they know us. We didn't want to change their opinions by telling them all the bad stuff we did before they "met" us.

But then we realized that was the whole point of being honest. Of course we want people to think good things about us, and we want people to recognize our accomplishments. But we don't want them to think we were born knowing how how to act right and make good choices. It was a process for us, one that started as soon as we realized we were going to be bringing another life into this world. By the time the cameras showed up, we were already trying as hard as we could to do right by the child we had on the way. But before that there were plenty of mistakes and bad choices and behavior that went on right up to the day we found out Catelynn was pregnant.

Think of how many "bad kids" out there have that potential to grow and change. You never know! There are a lot of kids out there who are born into the wrong environments, or don't know how to handle themselves when they're young, and sometimes it takes them longer to figure things out. But when you see one of those "bad kids," just remember, they might just be waiting for someone or something to help them be better. That's why we want people to know that we made that transformation. So we're being honest about the before and the after. Once upon a time, we were the "bad kids." But it's not a permanent label.

CHAPTER 3:

LIFE WITH DRUGS & ALCOHOL

Drugs and alcohol have had a huge impact on our lives. And we don't mean the times we messed around with them in our teenage years. We're talking generations of addiction, alcohol and drug abuse in both of our family histories. Throughout the lives of our parents, our grandparents and even our great-grandparents, drugs and alcohol have played a huge part in the cycle of addiction, poverty, and violence that we've worked so hard to break.

Wherever there's addiction, there's never just addiction. The addiction is just ground zero for destruction that spreads all across a person's life. It damages anyone who winds up in its path: friends, family, kids. Especially the kids. From the children who have to raise themselves because their parents are always high or passed out, to the ones who have to watch their family members getting wrestled into cop cars and carted off to prison, to the teenagers who grew up thinking being drunk and high is no big deal. We can barely scrape the surface. There's violence and abuse, screaming and fighting, dirty houses and scumbag grown-ups who don't give a crap if there's a five-year-old in the room when they're lighting up that crack pipe.

We've seen it all. We lived it. And it's a really sobering thing to look back at all our memories and realize how close we were to following in the wrong footsteps. We walked a thin, thin line, and we're grateful every day we didn't cross it.

It's All in the Family

Catelynn:

I don't know if I remember an exact age of when I realized my mom's drinking was a problem. I just know that for my whole life, for as long as I can remember, it was there. She'd drink too many beers, or there would be a party, and I would be the one watching the house to make sure everything was okay. We never talked about it. She was in denial for a long time. I was probably fifteen the first time I heard her admit that she was an alcoholic. My dad tells me she was a heavy drinker before I was born, so it was no secret. She just didn't call it what it was: alcoholism.

She definitely wasn't the first in her family. Her father has been an alcoholic for all of her life, and so far all of mine. And her mom had her share of things she did, too. Those are things everyone knows, but nobody ever brings up in detail. We know there's a history of addiction there, but no one confronts it like it's a problem. It just gets swept under the rug, except really you can still see it.

I know my mom's life was hurt by her parents' addictions, from the way she was treated to the irresponsible behavior she could never count on. And then there's the fear that comes with it, like the time her dad crashed his motorcycle on the way to pick her up from a friend's house, because he was so drunk. That kind of drama and danger is scary for a kid.

But they get used to it, and then they sometimes end up doing the same things. My mom started drinking around the time she got her driver's license, at about sixteen or seventeen. And from then on, drinking was a problem for her. It was a problem before I was born, and after I was born, and all through my life.

Children of alcoholics end up being caretakers instead of kids. There was always this burden on me to watch the house while she was too drunk, which felt like always. It was never just a few beers. If there was a case of beers in the fridge, she had to drink them all, and then she'd want to go out and get more. And the house was chaos all the time, because she couldn't keep things straight. She'd hide her keys from herself so she wouldn't be able to drive drunk, which was a good idea. But then she'd get so drunk she'd forget where the keys were, and then she'd be pissed because she couldn't find them!

And it was scary sometimes. When my mom passed out on the couch, you could not wake her up. I could shake her for thirty minutes, I could slap her in the face, but she was out cold. That's really terrifying for a little kid.

But even I never really confronted it for what it was, at least not for a long time. The first time I actually sat down and talked to my mom about her alcoholism about it was in couples' therapy. I hadn't been living with her for years, and I was never home if I could help it. I was always at Tyler's house, or a friend's house. I stayed away as much as possible. She was just so unpredictable. Sometimes she'd be so happy, and I hated when she would cling to me when she was drunk and hang on my shoulder. But as soon as I reacted, she'd turn into a complete bitch. It would change in a heartbeat.

It did end up getting a little better. She didn't stop drinking, but she worked not to get sloppy drunk. She married a guy who wasn't a big drinker, and that was a good influence.

Addiction is huge on my mom's side of the family. Her parents weren't even the ones who started it. They're all products of their environments, as far back as I can see. My grandma's dad, my great-grandfather, was an alcoholic to the day he died. We used to go visit him until he was in his seventies, and even then we always had to bring him booze. And there are more relatives, aunts and uncles and cousins, who have just destroyed themselves with alcohol or cocaine or meth. So everyone is repeating the same legacies of addiction, over and over. It just infects the family. And with it comes a lot of verbal and emotional abuse, which also trickles down and spreads.

All the bad behavior, that's what kids in the family are learning from day one. They grow up and make the same mistakes because they learned all the wrong crap about drugs and alcohol from their environment. That's how cycles work.

Memories of Violence

Tyler:

Drugs and violence were always connected in my head, thanks to my dad Butch and one crazy week I spent with him when I was eight. He'd just gotten out of prison that summer, and I was stoked to have my dad around. I wanted all the time I could spend with him.

He was staying with my uncle and my uncle's five kids, and they didn't care what went on. They just didn't give a shit what went on in front of the kids, and the kids were so young, we were oblivious to the details of their partying. We just thought, "This is how grownup guys hang out." I wasn't familiar with seeing anybody under the influence, really. My mom would drink at family reunions, but she'd never get drunk. My dad was the first one I saw go all out.

That week didn't end well. Why not? Well, one night they were all hanging out, drinking, playing cards, and this woman came in saying, "Butch! Butch! Somebody's there with a flashlight!" This was kind of a rough place, not the nicest part of town. It wasn't unusual for people to break into your car and steal your stuff or anything. And that's what everybody assumed this was. So of course my dad got all tough went stalking out there to whoop some ass, with me following behind, excited to see him lay the smackdown.

So I was right behind him when we saw the light from the flashlight, and then we heard the dogs barking. Three cops came out from behind the garage screaming, "Get down! Get down!" Four other cops came up from the driveway. They went after him hard. These cops were pissed off. They'd been looking for him for months, and when they got him, they didn't hold back. They jumped on him and smashed his face into the ground. I mean, smashed him down on the concrete. So when I saw that, I went crazy and ran at the cops. I was an eight year old kid going at the cops, thinking they were the bad guys.

Of course one of the officers grabbed me, and then my big sister came running out. She was four years older, so she had more memories of my dad. She kind of knew this was the kind of thing that happened if you got close to my dad. She put both her arms around me to try and pull me back. She was saying, "Tyler, don't look at this, just look at me. Mom's coming to get us." But I was screaming for my dad to look at me. I'll never forget that: He would not look at me. That was how I knew he was ashamed. He would not look at me. But that was all I wanted. That's why I got away from my sister and I ran after that cop car screaming, just wanting to see him turn around and look at me through the window.

That was a bad weekend. And all that was because of drugs. He broke into somebody's house and stole something to get some money to go out and buy his crack rocks. That's what happened.

My mom was pissed off. Not just because my dad had messed up so bad and made it so I had to see something like that, but also at him and my uncle for letting my cousins and me run wild in that environment. My uncle had caught my cousin and me smoking, and he came clean with my mom about it. She was just pissed. And knowing my mom, I think she was just as pissed at herself for not knowing better when she let me go over there.

But on the ride home, she talked to me. I was asking her tons of questions. I couldn't understand what my dad could have done to make those cops hate him so much, or why they'd done that to him, hurt him, and treated him like that. And she had to explain to her kid that my dad had an addiction, and it made him do things that hurt the people he cared about. "That's why you're hurt right now," she said. "He knows it's wrong, but he has a disease that makes him make these bad choices."

I was pissed. I thought the eight-year-old equivalent of, "Fuck that." Not only had my dad abandoned me for these drugs, but I had to see the cops bashing and smashing him like that. If I wasn't born with a problem with authority figures, I had a pretty freakin' big problem with them after that. That's how I went into second grade. That's when I started really fighting with teachers and getting suspended.

Catelynn:

There was a lot of violence like that around me, too. I had one uncle who had a huge meth problem. I can remember him hallucinating while I was at his house, asking him if I could see the government people flying around his house. He was always in some kind of trouble, in jail or getting bailed out. Once he went on a meth binge, got drunk, got in his car, crashed into a school bus, got caught with a gun he wasn't supposed to have, and got hauled off in handcuffs. But the worst was when he'd beat his wife in front of the kids. He'd freak out and start to whoop her ass in front of us, until she'd get away, throw us all in the truck and speed off to get away.

It was like scary movie stuff sometimes. One time, my mom had to go over there because he was screaming he was going to chop her head off with a machete! When she got there, there he was, actually standing there with a machete ready to chop her head off.

I wasn't safe from violent addicts, either. When I was thirteen or fourteen, Tyler and I suspected my mom's boyfriend at the time – the father of my little brother – was doing crack. We found proof when we found a crackpipe hidden in the bathroom, and three days after that, we found out we were suddenly being evicted.

Because my brother was just a little baby at the time, the landlord gave us a few extra days to pack up and leave. Tyler came over to help, and so he and my mom and my sister and I were packing up the whole house. The boyfriend, though, was just sitting in a chair watching, and he was obviously high on crack. He was running his mouth saying ridiculous stuff like, "We don't have to go anywhere! I paid everything! We don't have to pack, we're not leaving!" But my mom and I knew that wasn't true. We all just kept working while he sat around, high and talking crap. Then my mom left the house for a bit. While she was gone,

I made the mistake of making some remark to the boyfriend about him not helping us pack.

This guy just lost it. I mean, he lost it so bad he jumped out of his chair and I took off running. He chased me to the bathroom, with Tyler running right behind him. My sister got so scared she had run ahead of me to hide in the shower, so she was in there screaming when he caught up with me. This man picked me up by the neck, threw me to the ground, and pinned me down on the floor between the toilet and the shower and started choking me. I was trying to kick him and punch him, and my sister was screaming bloody murder. Tyler got some burst of Hulk strength and pulled the guy off of me, and we shut the door and called 911. The cops came and took him off to jail. My mom fell apart over that, crying, "How could he lay a hand on my kid? How can I ever be with him again?"

Tyler:

I don't know how that happened. He's a big guy and I was just this scrawny little fourteen-year-old. But when your girlfriend's getting attacked by somebody you go into panic mode. Adrenaline, or something.

That was the first time we looked at each other and said, "Something seriously wrong is going on." We find a crack pipe in the bathroom and three days later they're getting evicted and she's got this guy choking her on the bathroom floor. Obviously something in that household was not right. I mean, that's an understatement.

Catelynn:

Right after that, we had to move to a really bad part of Detroit, right on 7 Mile and Mound, which is a horrible place to live. Our next door neighbor was named Fats. He was a drug dealer and had his four-year-old kid dropping dime bags out the window, like a druggie drive-through. We went to bed hearing gunshots. It was awful. We could barely even go outside. So I got out of there every weekend I could. Tyler and his mom would come to pick me up all the time, just to get me out of there.

First Tastes

Tyler:

The first time I tried cigarettes, drinking, and weed was that week at my dad's house. Yep, I was eight. I got into everything with my cousin. He was the same age as me, and we ran wild around that house while my dad and my uncle and all their friends were doing whatever they were doing. No supervision. So, big surprise, one day we came across one of my uncle's bags of weed. We basically knew what it was, but we didn't know what to do with it. We knew how to poke holes in a pop can to smoke it, but we didn't know how to break it up or anything, so we kind of just stuck it on top and burned it. Either way, it's the thought that counts. I was toking up when I was eight years old.

Catelynn and I were both smoking a lot of pot when we got together. And once we were dating, we did it with each other all the time. We messed around with pretty much anything we could get our hands on — not the hard stuff, but the usual bad junior high kid stuff. For example, air duster. We went through a huge phase of huffin' air duster. I'd go into CVS and steal four cans of air duster for us to huff.

That stuff is serious. I can't tell you how many times I've seen friends collapse and lie on the ground in their own blood for hours after huffin' air duster. Someone could punch you in the face when you were on air duster. All you can hear is this "WOM-WOM-WOM" sound. It feels all tingly, but you're out of control of your body. You feel your head turn into a balloon. You feel light and heavy at the same time. Out of every drug I've ever done, it was the most intense high and the most messed up thing I've ever done in my life. Everyone should be scared of that shit.

Once I woke up after huffing too much air duster, and I was lying on the floor with chunks of foam coming out of my mouth. I was like, "What happened, dude?" All my friends were so wrecked on air duster they were laughing. They said I started having a seizure and shaking around on the ground, that my eyes rolled back in my head. I even pissed myself. I was so freaked out I had to leave. I thought about it all the way home.

Catelynn:

The first time I saw someone doing drugs, not just alcohol, was probably when I was ten. I could smell marijuana in the house. I didn't see it, but I smelled it. Of course that was one of the first things I ended up getting into when I was a little older.

We used to get high on the sleeping pill Unisom. We'd pop five or six Unisom and totally trip out. Our feet felt like cement, we couldn't move, and we hallucinated all this stuff on the walls. Other times we'd snort Ritalin or whatever other pill was on hand to try. And there was Robotrippin', where we chugged a bunch of cough syrup to get high. We did Ecstasy when we had that. Basically, anything we could get our hands on to get high with, we'd do it.

I was a little behind on the air duster. I watched my friends do it for about a month, but I was kind of scared of it. But then I got curious to see what the big deal was, so I started doing that, too.

We never really drank much, funny enough. We did everything else we could get, huffin', snorting pills, smoking weed, we were all about that stuff. But even our friends weren't really drinking. Why drink when you can huff air duster?

The stuff was crazy, though. Once my friend Sam and I were riding our bikes in the trailer park while huffing air duster. I huffed some, and then I got on my bike to ride away. Next thing I knew, I was lying on my back on the street with rain pouring down on me. That freaked me out. I didn't even know how long I'd been there. I could have been run over.

Tyler:

We used to have this friend whose mom and boyfriend were...well, kind of freaky people. We used to call them "Mom and Mike." She was this forty-year-old woman, and she'd let us do whatever we wanted in her house. Not only that, though. She'd push drugs on us. She'd offer us booze and offer us pills and offer us crack. All these fourteen-year-old kids were in this house, and she'd offer it like cookies. "Who wants to try crack?" "I do, I do!"

I never smoked crack, though, even while my friends were doing it, because my dad was a crackhead, and I wasn't about that. But one day she asked if I wanted to try "cocaine." I thought, sure, why not? I snort Ritalin and Adderall, what the hell? So I stayed up all night snorting coke with this old woman, coloring crazy shit in coloring books. And I remember waking up that morning and my first thought being, "I want more." There was this crazy moment where I would have done anything to get it. But luckily, a lightbulb came on, and I got up and left.

After that I told myself I'd never do cocaine again. I was freaked out by how bad I wanted it, and I was like, I'll never touch that again. I was even scared to tell Catelynn I'd done it in the first place, because Catelynn was totally against it. So I wasn't going to tell her, but my sister ratted me out.

Catelynn freaked. She told me she'd break up with me if I ever did it again. She told me, "My life got destroyed by this stuff. My mom's life was destroyed. I won't date somebody who does this stuff." And then suddenly I realized crack and cocaine are basically the same thing, and that stuff had destroyed my dad's life and my life, too. That flicked the switch. I wasn't gonna mess around with it anymore. So that was the last time I ever did it.

Catelynn:

Mom and Mike got me, too. One time I was at that house and she offered me some kind of anti-psychotic medication. I took it without thinking much of it, because I was doing dumb things at that time, and I'd taken tons of pills. So I swallowed this pill, and then sat around with all these forty-something-year-old people. I remember we smoked two blunts. And then all of a sudden I woke up on the floor, shaking, and my head hurt really, really bad. All of them were standing around me going, "Oh my god, are you okay? Are you okay?" Apparently I was standing there in the living room and I just lost consciousness and fell over backwards, smacked the back of my head right on the floor. I wandered out of there, but I couldn't even go home, I was so messed up. I had to stay at my friend Sam's and sleep it off on his couch.

Tyler:

All the neighborhood kids stopped going over there after awhile. It got old. They always felt like since they were providing all these drugs, they could treat the kids however they wanted. They ended up moving away after awhile. It was very strange.

Catelynn:

Over the years I think I've seen drugs and addiction cause so much damage. I've seen people acting crazy and forgetting what's even normal. After everything went down with that crackhead boyfriend of my mom's, she ended up getting back together with him when he came around saying he was dying. He came up with some fake hospital papers to prove he had some disease and he only had two years to live. He was my little brother's dad, after all, and she was thinking, "Well my son needs to know who he is, he only has two years to live." But it was a total lie. He was a con artist and a schemer and a pathological liar.

Growing up with all of that, seeing all that bad stuff as a kid, is the reason I've never even touched hard drugs. I smoked weed, I dabbled in a little alcohol, and I've done all the typical teenager drugs. That's not supposed to downplay them, but you know. The pot, the air duster, the ecstasy, those were all things people pretty typically dibbled and dabbled in back then. They were little phases for me. But I never touched the hard stuff, because I'd seen what it could do.

Closing Thoughts

Alcoholism and drug addiction have destroyed people in both our families for generations. We talk a lot about breaking the cycle, and that means understanding the cycle itself. What mistakes do we avoid? How did these problems get the best of the people we see around us? It's crazy to hear some of the things our parents went through before they had us, and what even our grandparents went through. We see all this damage caused to aunts and uncles and cousins and it always traces back to another parent with a drinking or drug problem. And looking at the ones who got out and did better, you don't see the drugs and alcohol taking up a big part of their lives.

We always had that in mind. We thought about our limits and we always told ourselves not to go too far. There was a hint of maturity there, even in the bad kid days, that came from seeing all that destruction and wanting to move far away from it.

We just wanted something different than what we had. And lucky for us, we had a few people in our lives who'd made the same decision. We each had somebody pushing us to do things with our lives, either a parent or a grandparent, to counteract the bad examples we were getting. Maybe that was all we needed to boost whatever in us that made us think, "We're not going to be like that. Not like them. We're gonna be different."

Still, obviously we weren't perfect. It would have been better not to mess around with air duster and snort cocaine in middle school. No doubt about that. And we can never be certain how long that phase would have lasted, if it wasn't for one little thing. Once that pregnancy test came back positive, there was no more room for drugs and alcohol in our lives. We dropped that stuff and didn't even have time to look back.

CHAPTER 4:

FROM TEEN SEX TO TEEN PREGNANCY

Sooner or later everyone probably experiences an event so important and meaningful that they start to look at their life in terms of before and after. So far everything you've read in this book took place in our "before," back when we were just another couple of poor Michigan kids stumbling (and huffing) our way through teenagerdom. Sure, we had a sense of wanting to grow up and become something more, but we hadn't really figured out how yet. Neither of us had any real plans for life except for whatever we were doing on any given day. There wasn't any meaning yet.

Back then, we were pretty reckless: about drugs, about getting into fights, about stealing. And guess what? We were kind of reckless about sex, too. We didn't mean to be. We sort of thought we knew what we were doing, to be honest. And that was probably half the problem.

Your first experiences with sex are huge, and they can have some serious effects on you. As kids grow up and take in more and more information about sex from the world around them, they start to develop their own outlooks, identities, and values. Some kids are more curious than others about sex, and some are so curious it's downright disturbing. Others don't seem to be interested at all, or have ideas what's appropriate and what's not. And, as much as people hate to talk about it, a lot of kids have learned way too much, way too soon.

We got together with totally different outlooks and backgrounds as far as sex was concerned. But we both ended up on the same wild ride. Our decision to have sex — and the way we handled it — brought about a consequence that changed our lives forever. In a way, sex and pregnancy are what created "before" and "after."

Tyler:

Catelynn and I got together by holding hands, but for months and months that was pretty much as far as it went. She was a virgin and had no interest in rushing into sex.

I was the complete opposite, and that wasn't a good thing. I had actually been dating girls since grade school, and I'd broken up with them for not wanting to fool around. In the fourth grade, I got suspended for pushing a girl against a locker and trying to kiss her. Looking back on it, it's horrifying. Why was I such a hypersexual kid? Well, all I know is it started when I was nine.

The older girl who molested me was a friend of my older sister. She was about four years older than me, which is a big difference at that age. One day I went over to her house with my sister and some other people, and for some reason or another, everyone else left but this older girl and me. For the next several hours, while we were alone together in her house, it was sex act after sex act after sex act. It went on all day. She had us doing everything she could think of, one thing after another. There'd be a break and then it would start up again. And when it was finally over, I didn't know what the hell had happened.

My reaction was to brag about it with all my friends. I think I was trying to get a reaction out of them to help me understand what to make of it. As young as I was, I had some sense that what happened wasn't right. But I didn't have many ways to process something so crazy. And my bragging didn't work out. One day I was at a barbecue and I started talking to two girls about it. They knew immediately that something wasn't right, and they went and told someone. When it got back to my mom, she freaked out. She thought I was lying or saying dirty things to those girls, and I think it scared her. That day she pulled me aside and smacked me for it.

After that, it turned into this very ugly, awkward kind of thing with other adults hearing about it and being concerned. That's what clued me in that what had happened was wrong. My mom and I never talked about it again until much later, when I was older and we went to counseling. I think she just didn't know what to do. Neither did I. Things are weird when boys are molested by girls. People think about it differently. The message you get is that it's a cool thing to happen, something to brag about. Then on the other hand you learn adults don't want you to talk about it.

It wasn't cool at all. It made me think sex was something kids could do, which influenced me to act too sexual when I was too young. Before long I was breaking up with my little girlfriends because they were prudes. Prudes! We were ten-year-olds! It's so messed up.

I wound up finding a girlfriend who wanted to do it all the time. She was crazy, and that was basically all we did. Going from her to Catelynn was a real shocker. But I never thought about dumping Cate for holding back. There was something about her self-respect and the way she just came right out and said "no" that almost compelled me to want to get closer to her. Cate was really good for me in that way.

Catelynn:

Yes, I was a prude. I wasn't having any of that. I was a little punk, but I was a classy punk! I was a virgin when I met Tyler, and I didn't see any reason to throw that away for no reason. He'd obviously had more experience than me and had different ideas about sex, but that was his deal. I had other boyfriends before him, but I didn't do anything with them at all. I've just always been the kind of girl who respects my body.

I never liked to show it off in skimpy clothes or anything, and I didn't feel like giving it up to some guy just because he wanted it that second.

Tyler really wanted to have sex, but I made him wait for about nine months. I never worried that he'd dump me like he'd dump those other girls. Not because I was sure he wouldn't, but because if he did, that would just mean he wasn't the right guy for me. It was that simple. I wasn't going to compromise my self-respect.

And it was worth it, because he waited. Instead of having sex we hung out and talked, and talked, and talked. We built a really strong relationship without that one thing. And then one night, when we were fooling around in his room, I just said, "Are you gonna do it already, or not?"

Tyler was like, "What?" He was so shocked when I suggested it, all of a sudden he was the one who wasn't sure! He kept asking me, "Do you really want to do this? Are you absolutely sure? Are you sure you want to?" So in the end I was the one saying, come on, let's just do it!

Once we'd done it once, we were doing it all the time! After waiting so long we turned into crazy, horny teenagers. It was so bad. We would drink and party together and fool around constantly, all the time.

Oh, the stories. Tyler's mom had this camper parked by her house that we used to hang out in sometimes. One night we went out there with some booze and started drinking. Once we were good and buzzed, of course we ended up banging in his mom's trailer. We were having a good old time until we heard her come outside and yell his name.

"Tyler! What on earth are you doing?"

We just froze and stared at each other, and then Tyler jumped up and yelled, "We're just talking!"

His mom wasn't fooled! "Put your clothes on and get out here!"

It wasn't until later that we realized we were in the camper with the lights on and she could see everything! Thank God we were drunk, or we'd have to remember that incident sober.

Tyler:

All those months of waiting paid off, but unfortunately, we were not being safe at all. We were using the pull-out method, and that was it.

I didn't wear condoms and Cate never went on birth control. We just didn't feel like we had to. My parents hadn't given me a real talk about it yet, and Cate's parents hadn't given her a talk. We went through sex education and everything, but I sort of thought I was an expert already. We thought pulling out is good enough, and like typical dumb kids, we couldn't actually comprehend what would happen if it wasn't.

We can't blame anybody, but I wish someone would have hammered it in a little harder. We just approached sex like we'd taken the pills and the air duster. It was fun and it was available, so we did it, because the risks didn't really scare us. We were doing adult things with a child's level of understanding.

Catelynn:

Now we believe it's really important to talk to kids as much as possible about sex. We don't exactly believe in abstinence-only education. It would be nice if everyone could be abstinent, but the fact is, most teenagers aren't. You can tell the teenagers of the world to stop having sex as much as you want, but they're going to do it. You'll never have a world where teenagers are not having sex. So you can still teach them that abstinence is the safest thing to do, but you also have to make sure they understand that when they do have sex they can do it in a safe and healthy way. That means condoms and also having control over your own decisions. We want to teach people, "It's your body, it's your choice, and you don't have to do anything without protecting yourself." If you're going to do it, be smart about it. Don't be stupid.

A Major Consequence

Catelynn:

I didn't ever suspect that I was pregnant. One day I was cleaning the shower and I suddenly got really sick. The door was closed, and I just thought, "Wow, I probably shouldn't have locked myself in a room with all these cleaning supplies." I didn't feel good for a couple of days. I couldn't hold anything down, not even water. And I had my period, so

I ruled out pregnancy right away. That was the first thing my mom asked me on the way to the doctor. I told her I needed to go because I might have the flu, and she was asking me if I was sure I wasn't pregnant. I was like no, mom, geez. I'm on my period. I just think I have the flu.

So they hooked me up to an IV, had me pee in a cup, asked me if I was pregnant, and I said, "No, I'm not pregnant." Then I lay there for awhile, with my mom sitting in the room with me, waiting to hear from the doctor again.

When she came back in, she didn't say anything except, "Well, you're pregnant." Then she walked out.

I can't explain why, but my feeling was instant rage. I just wanted to get out of there. I was like, Get this IV out of my arm, and let me get out of this place. My mom got the papers from the doctor and we got out of there. She drove straight to Tyler's house.

Tyler:

I knew Catelynn was going to the hospital, but I thought the same thing she did. I didn't think she was pregnant. I was hanging out with friends of mine while she was at the doctor, and they were giving me all this shit. "Dude, what if she's pregnant? Dude!"

"Whatever," I thought.

Then Cate and her mom pull up. So I go out to the car, and she's lying in the backseat. I get in with her and have her lie down on my lap. Her mom doesn't say a word, just hands me a bunch of papers and starts driving.

Catelynn doesn't say anything, either. So I look at the papers and at first I don't understand them, because it's all this medical mumbo-jumbo. But I read, read, read all this stupid stuff, until I get to the bottom.

Pregnancy Test: Positive.

"No."

I felt like I was going to throw up. I barely even remember the car ride back to Catelynn's house, but I know it was silent. I didn't know what to say. I just stared out the window with my chin on my hand, thinking, "What am I going to do now?"

Catelynn had already moved ten times that year and they were in a new trailer with no furniture set up yet. It was this empty place. You could hear the echoes as you talked. All Cate had in her room was a mattress on the floor. She lay down and closed her eyes, and I just sat down against the wall beside her in shock. I didn't know what to do.

My first reaction was, "You're going to do this, you're going to have a child." And then I was thinking, "This can't happen to me. How can this be happening?" I looked at Cate and I just thought, "I don't know what to do."

It was an intense, draining, emotional day.

An Extreme Decision: Abortion, Parenthood, or Something Else?

Catelynn:

I was so overwhelmed and upset that I slept that whole day. My mom woke me up at six the next morning and the first thing she said was, "Do you want an abortion?"

I had always been against abortion. But you never know how you'll really react until you're in that situation. I was young and I was absolutely terrified. I broke down crying and said yeah, yeah, yeah. People say that they'll do a certain thing, but when I was caught off guard, woken up like that and still shocked and scared, that was how I reacted.

Tyler:

Cate's mom called me up and asked if I could skip school the next day. And I said, "Sure, I guess, what's tomorrow?" She said, "I made Cate an appointment, we're gonna get an abortion."

I said, "Hang on, just wait a second. We need to think about this." I didn't know how to process that. But it was my baby, too, and I didn't want to make any big decisions I didn't understand. I told Catelynn's mom we needed to take some time so we could all think it over and discuss what was going to happen. After I hung up I just sat there trying to untangle my thoughts. I was sure I wasn't ready to be a father, but I didn't like the sound of an abortion, either.

I didn't have a clear understanding of the issue or anything. I didn't really know anything about it. I spent all day researching everything about abortion. I talked to a teacher I trusted and he helped me find trustworthy medical websites I could learn from. I wanted to see what the procedure actually was, what they'd do, and how things were different in different weeks, what the risks were and all of that.

So I printed it all out and went over to her house to talk about it with her. I thought, she's going to be the one who has to do this. Her body will carry the baby and she's the one who would go through pregnancy and birth. I wanted her to make the decision but I wanted her to know everything she could know to make the best decision for herself.

She looked at one page and immediately said, "No. Absolutely not. I can't do this. We're going to have to think about something else."

And that was really when the whole ball started rolling on the idea of adoption.

It still wasn't an easy choice between parenthood and placing the baby for adoption. Catelynn and I bounced back and forth: I wanted to parent and she wanted adoption, she wanted to parent and I wanted adoption. We did this over and over, just figuring things out from every angle we could. But when you're in that situation, you're thinking with pure emotion and pure feeling. You're all wrapped up in yourself and what you're feeling, what you want that second. You have to step back and think logically.

So I finally wrote up a "pros and cons" list of what I could give this child as a parent, versus what adoption could do for her. Before I started the list I thought it would be a tough balance. But what happened was that the one thing I had on the side for parenting the child was, "being with biological family and surrounded by love." That was literally the only thing I could think of. The cons were, "You don't have a diploma. You don't have a license. You don't have a cell phone. You don't have money. You have two years of high school left. You have no way of getting a car..." When I looked at all the things on the cons side, it was like, "Holy shit." Votes for adoption were huge. She still gets surrounded by love. She gets her own room. Catelynn was living in a trailer! The crib would be in Catelynn's room! There was just no way, logically, that it would work.

So what I did was I left the list on her dresser and I went home. Later that night she called me and said, "Let's do it. Let's make an appointment with an adoption counselor."

Catelynn:

The list brought us back to the reality of what we could actually provide for a child. It wasn't about us or what we wanted. We couldn't think about our own wishes. It was about the child, the child's needs, and what was best for the child. I wanted to think of more things we could give her, too. And the same thing happened to me. All I could think of was living with biological parents, unconditional love. So I thought, let's look into adoption and see if it's the right thing for us or not. But even then it was hard.

Tyler:

We knew we didn't have good enough reasons to choose parenthood. Yeah, it could work. We could scrape by. We could live paycheck to paycheck and struggle our whole lives. But we both knew that the one fact of "biological family" was not enough to give this child the best chance.

Still, it was so hard to separate the facts from the emotions. As teenagers, we wanted to be selfish. We wanted to do what would make us happy. And we wanted to parent that child. That was something we really, really wanted. But every time we thought about the nitty-gritty, we realized it was something we were wanting for ourselves.

Catelynn:

It really was an everyday fight to put our emotions aside. Every time we thought about what we wanted, we'd have to pull ourselves back in our head and think, "But it's not about what we want. What does she deserve?" It wasn't about what we thought we deserved.

But ever since I was little, I was the girl who wanted to be a mom. I wanted to be a wife. I wanted to take care of my children and husband. Ever since I can remember, I've just always wanted to be a mother. That made the decision excruciating. Because in a way, being pregnant was a lifelong dream. And I had to pull myself out of my emotions to face the fact that it was not the right time, and I knew it.

One night I was so torn about it, I started praying: "God, if I'm supposed to choose adoption, if this is the right choice, I need peace in this decision. I need a sign." I talked to God in my bedroom for about an hour until I fell asleep. And you know what? The next morning in the car on my way to school, adoption commercials started coming on the radio. When I got to class and started on vocabulary, I saw the words "adoption" and "birth parents."

I was like, well, thank you. There's my sign. That was all I needed. And that was the moment on I made peace with my decision. I thought, "That's it. I'm gonna do this, and I don't care who the hell tries to get in my way."

Tyler:

I know it was hard for Cate as the mother. She's always had a strong maternal instinct. Even her dad has told me about how she always wanted to help animals and rescue baby birds. She was always very nurturing and she always dreamed of being a mom. But she set her own wants aside to provide this child with the best possible life. Once she told me, "I remember crying and thinking about being a mom and going through all the struggles. And then I would stop crying and feel peace when I thought about Carly being adopted. And that's how I knew that was what I wanted to do."

Less than one percent of women choose adoption for their babies. Ninety-nine percent of women who parent choose to get pregnant or have an abortion. That's why it's so ironic and amazing that Catelynn chose adoption, because for someone who had dreamed about parenthood for so long and had such a strong maternal instinct, it was the ultimate sacrifice. She's in that one percent of women who made that decision.

Catelynn:

My mom was dead set against adoption. People find that surprising sometimes, because she'd been willing to take me in for an abortion. I think she was able to think about abortion because it still feels so unreal early on in the pregnancy. But in her generation, adoption was a bad and scary thing. Nobody really knew about it. There was adoption within our family, where people would adopt their kids out to other relatives, but I wasn't going to do that. In her mind I was going to give birth to her granddaughter and then send her away forever.

Tyler:

My dad was totally against the adoption, too. And as we'll tell you, they combined forces to fight us all the way through. Not everyone approved. And we have had people tell us we took the easy way out. But whoever thinks placing your child for adoption is the easy way out... that's just ignorant. If anything, having the child would have been the easy way out. That's how it was done in our families, that's what they wanted, and that's what we knew. Or we could have had the abortion, that would have been the easy way out. For us, adoption was the highest expression of love we could offer.

Tyler:

It's weird to look back on all of the crazy shit we did, to think about how this one thing could completely change us and our maturity and morality.

Catelynn:

Shoot, we acted crazy up until the day we found out. And then there was a child growing inside of me, and that just changed everything.

Closing Thoughts

No teenagers should have to make the difficult decision we had to make. No adult should, either. But hey, teens, we're talking to you in particular: Be smart! You can get condoms. There's no reason to risk putting yourselves in the position we ended up in. The only positive pregnancy test you ever want to see is one you're actively hoping and planning for. Be safe, use protection, or wait to have sex until you're ready to do it responsibly. And if you're not ready for sex at all? Don't have it! You are in control of that decision. Don't ever let anyone tell you otherwise, and don't ever let anyone convince you that it's not worth it to take precautions against pregnancy.

Parents, talk to your kids! We know you might not like to think of your kids having sex at all. And by all means, tell them not to if that's what you want to do! But we strongly suggest you also make sure they know it's not an all or nothing decision. Abstinence might be the best choice, but if your teenager does end up choosing to have sex, as many, many teenagers do, we hope they know they don't have to do it recklessly. Ultimately, those intimate decisions will be in their hands. We can only hope that they have all the knowledge they can possibly have to help them make the choice and handle it in the best way possible.

Cate and I didn't plan on pregnancy. And once it happened, the last thing we wanted to do was make this huge, painful decision. No teenager is prepared for that, and no mother or father is naturally inclined to consider a choice as drastic as full-time parenthood or adoption. For us, as naturally selfish teenagers, deciding to place our daughter for adoption would be (and still is) the hardest decision we have ever made. Nobody *wants* to go through the intense grief and loss that are involved in that process. No one wants to make such a giant sacrifice. But once you're pregnant, it doesn't matter what you want anymore. Carelessly following your own desires is what gets you into that situation in the first place! Once you're pregnant, every decision you make has to be about that baby.

No child is asked to be brought into this world and no child picks and chooses his or her parents. A child relies on its parents to provide the life they deserve. If you're not sure you can provide that life, be safe and do what you can so that you never get stuck with such a dilemma in the first place!

CHAPTER 5:

A BETTER LIFE
FOR A CHILD

Making the decision was only the beginning. When we chose to place our child for adoption, we knew we were in for an emotional journey. What else could it be? Make no mistake: We wished more than anything in the world that we could parent this baby. We dreamed about it day in and day out. But at the end of every dream was the harsh realization that we couldn't give her what we wanted to give her. There was absolutely nothing we could do to guarantee this baby the safe and happy home that we desperately wanted to provide.

That was an emotional battle we had to face. But what we didn't know was that some of the people we counted on would turn against us. See, not everyone was proud of us for making this choice. And the ones who disagreed went to unbelievable lengths to undermine our decision, challenge our courage, and sabotage our plans. From the first call to the adoption counselor all the way to the delivery room, we had to charge head-on through every layer of dysfunction in our homes, our families, and our lives.

Each of us had a parent who supported our decision. And each of us had a parent who could not have been more adamantly against it. Unfortunately for us, the ones who stood against us were completely united with each other. Because right before we found out about the pregnancy, our own respective dysfunctional parents decided they were in love with each other.

We were in for a hell of a rough ride.

Two Houses United, Two Families Divided

Tyler:

Never in a million years did I expect my father to start dating my girlfriend's mom.

Catelynn:

I saw it coming a mile away. As soon as Tyler's dad got out of prison the second time, as soon as I met him, I thought, "Oh, no. He is exactly my mom's type." I tried to tell Tyler there would be trouble if they ever came across each other. I said, "Tyler, we cannot let them meet." Tyler didn't get it. He thought I was crazy.

Tyler:

I really didn't sense the danger of them getting together. All I could think was, "I'm pretty sure your mom can resist an ex-con straight out of prison. Why would she jump for a guy like that?" But Catelynn would just shake her head and say, "I'm telling you, Tyler. I'm telling you. I don't want them to meet."

Then one day I was visiting with him, and Catelynn came over with her mom to pick me up. I introduced my dad to her mom. Sure enough, the next thing you know, sparks were flying and it was happening. Cate-lynn was totally one hundred percent right.

It was still confusing to me, because from where we were standing it was such an obviously bad idea. But at the same time, I felt where Catelynn's mom was coming from. Like I've said, my dad's a very good talker. He can make almost anything sound really good, regardless of whether or not it is.

As soon as it started up, I looked for a chance to try and talk Cate's mom out of it. I waited until she was sober, pulled her aside, and said, "I'm telling you right now: You do not wanna be with this guy." I told her about all of the drugs, the jail time, and all of the other things he'd done. I told her he'd talked out of his ass for his whole life, he was completely unreliable, he was an addict, he wasn't capable of holding up a relationship. I told her all this over the course of a forty-five minute conversation. But she already had the hearts in her eyes, and it was just in one ear and out the other.

Catelynn:

Watching my mom on TV, people don't get the best impression of her. Sometimes it seems like she's just home drunk all the time. That's not the case at all. She's an addict, but she's always worked her ass off to have her own money and a place to live where she wasn't leaning on a man to cover the bills. But at the same time, she hated to be alone, and she didn't always pick the best guys. And that's putting it lightly. In the case of Tyler's dad, she wasn't even his only girlfriend! She was the side-chick! Most women would not have put up with that. But she was so invested in him, so fast, that she said, "I'll wait for him! I'll wait for him to pick me!"

Obviously a major part of their connection was that they were both partiers.

Tyler:

My dad told Cate's mom from the beginning that he was not a one-woman man. He was a player and he made it clear from the get-go. And I tried to make it clear to her that he was being honest. But as it turned out, the other girlfriend was not so into the drugs and the partying. She was another woman who deserved better, but the difference was that she knew it. She had her own business and didn't want to mess up her life.

So my dad turned toward the woman he knew would put up with all the wild stuff, and that was Cate's mom. He knew he could get high and come home and she wouldn't care. He saw a chance to do what he wanted with no consequences, so he went for it. Plus, Cate's mom could keep up. It was more fun.

Catelynn:

They hadn't even been dating for more than a couple of months when we moved into the new trailer. And then, all of a sudden, Tyler's dad was staying there every day. I said, "Mom, what the hell? I thought no one was moving in!" She told me he was just staying for a little while. But sure as shit, within a couple of weeks, he'd moved in.

One day we came home and they were both drunk at the kitchen table. As soon as we walked in they threw up their arms, gave us these big grins, and announced that they were getting married.

"Sure, drunk-asses." We assumed it was just the booze talking, or it was a joke. But the joke was on us. The next time we came home, they had a freaking marriage license. They'd only been together for three or four months. We never even had time to talk them out of it.

We were freaking out. We knew it wasn't going to last forever, but we also knew there'd be trouble for as long as it did. They were addicts, and their relationship was the perfect environment for their worst habits to come out. As it turned out, they stayed married for six years. Every one of those years was bad news. But the main thing that came out of the first year was that they turned on us.

Tyler:

We were sixteen years old. Catelynn was pregnant. In just a handful of months, she was going to give birth to our baby. And during those months, we had to wrap our minds and hearts around the decision to place that baby for adoption. No matter which way you looked at it, we were two scared, overwhelmed kids who were about as emotionally vulnerable as you could imagine. If we had ever needed the full love and support of our parents, we needed it right then.

But instead of being there for us, my dad and Cate's mom joined forces to fight us tooth and nail all the way through. They fought us at home, they fought us in court. From the day we decided to make an adoption plan to the day we said goodbye to our newborn daughter, my dad and Cate's mom did everything they could to stand in our way.

It's Not Easy to Break the Cycle

Catelynn:

Our situation was horrible, but it wasn't exactly rare. Even when adoption is obviously the best choice, there's no end to the number of people who will try to talk the birth parents out of it. There are a lot of reasons behind that opposition, and it's different for every situation. Adoption isn't just emotional for the birth parents. It can bring up a lot of difficult feelings for the extended birth family, too. Clashing values and misconceptions about adoptions are just a couple pieces of the puzzle.

Just think about how we made our decision. We put our life under a microscope and shined a light on every single way it fell short. And our conclusion was that our situation wasn't acceptable for our child. We didn't mean that as an attack on our parents, but it's obvious how it could bring up some really complicated and difficult emotions. Unfortunately, that's exactly the kind of situation that can trigger an addict. So during this whole thing, my mom's drinking got worse and worse. That just intensified the conflict and caused even more of a rift, which made it impossible to work things out. At the same time, it reinforced the reasons we chose adoption in the first place.

I have sympathy for everything that my mom went through. It's not a mystery to me why she wasn't the perfect person, or the perfect parent. The fact is that no matter what her flaws are, she raised me with a ton of love and we were best friends until this came between us. I was devastated not to have her support. Never in a million years did I think she'd turn her back on me when I needed her most. But that's what happened. I think both my pregnancy and my decision to get an adoption pushed her over the edge and back into the bottle. And that's when we went from being good friends to fighting all the time. By the time we were on TV, that's basically what people saw.

Really, all the conflict stemmed back to the fact that I was trying to break the cycle. When I got pregnant, I was repeating something that had happened for previous generations in my family. My grandma was a young mom, and her life was chaos. And then my mom was a young mom, and her life was chaos. And then I became a young mom, but I stomped on the cycle.

When I chose adoption, I was going against all of their decisions. I was coming right out and saying, "I'm not going to do what you did. I want to do better." I didn't do it to declare war on them or judge them. But they could tell I was putting space between my life and theirs, and they didn't like it.

It's not easy to break the cycle.

Tyler:

What amazed me was the way my dad could look me in the eye and lecture me about "manning up" and "taking responsibility for your child." Just take a minute to think about the memories I've shared about my dad, and let that soak in.

My decision to place my child for adoption wasn't about laziness or cowardice. It wasn't about turning my back on my responsibilities. It was about loving that child and doing the right thing. I wanted to parent that baby. Catelynn wanted to parent that baby. But no sane person could look at Catelynn's and my situation, look at the wonderful adult couples who'd been approved for adoption, and say, "Oh, that baby is definitely better off in the trailer with the broke high school kids." Give me a break.

The problem was that this was a major difference in values between me and Catelynn, and my dad and her mom. Remember, when Cate and I wrote out the pros and cons of parenting this baby, the one thing on the pro side was "living with biological parents." For us, that one reason was obliterated by all the cons. But to my dad and Cate's mom, it was the exact opposite. In their eyes, it didn't matter how many cons piled up: "You don't give away your blood."

"You don't give away your blood. You never give away your blood." I heard that over and over from my dad. My dad, who'd never been around. My dad, who'd been in jail for most of his life. My dad, who chose crack cocaine over his family and did it over and over and over again.

"You don't give away your blood," he'd boom at me. "I don't care what you have to do. I don't care how worried you are about money. I'd go door to door begging for food if I had to. I'd sleep in my car before I'd give up my kid."

"You'd subject your kid to that life?" I said. It was so hypocritical I couldn't even believe it. "Just because *you* don't agree with adoption? What about the kid? What part of that has anything to do with being a father and taking care of your child?"

"I don't care," he said. "*You never give away your blood.*"

When I couldn't take it anymore, I called him out. I told him, "You did give up your kid. You gave me up when you chose drugs and crime and jail over me. If you think I'm taking parenting advice from a crackhead, you're insane. You know what, dad? Whatever advice you live by, I'm pretty sure I should do the opposite."

No, it's not easy to break the cycle. If it was, the world would be very different. But the more these bad influences tried to talk us into doing what they would do, the more we believed in our decision. Their opposition made us stronger. It told us we were doing the right thing.

Bad Memories, Hard Lessons

Catelynn:

Did I want to be a mom? Yes. More than anything in the entire world, I wanted to be a wife and a mom. But my dream was to take care of my family. And that takes more than love. Love was never what was missing. I had endless love for the child inside of me, just like my mom had endless love for me. But love didn't save me from the instability I hated so much growing up. If I parented my baby, I would shower her with love every single day. But how could I protect her from the things I'd seen?

I'd never experienced stability in my entire life. I'd moved more than ten times. I'd been attacked by crackheads. I'd been surrounded by drug deals and violence and hard times for as long as I could remember. And yes, there was love and happiness mixed up in all that, and parents who did the best they could. But all I had to do was think back over the last couple of years of my life to know I wanted better for my daughter.

Just look at what had happened with my mom's crackhead boyfriend, the one who scammed his way back into the family after he attacked me. If our lives had been more stable and secure, we wouldn't have gotten stuck moving to Detroit with him. But thanks to the way things were, my mom got sucked into a bad situation, and so did her kids.

Living in that neighborhood in Detroit was like being stuck in an episode of Cops. There were drug deals going on everywhere you looked. There were gunshots at night. Needless to say, there wasn't a chance in hell I was going to go to high school there. My mom didn't want me going, either. Detroit public schools are not the place to be, and definitely not for me. I was tough, but I was still just a small-town white girl from the trailer park. I knew I wouldn't last five minutes. The only kids in the neighborhood I made friends with ended up scaring the shit out of me. There was a house full of teenagers two doors down from us, and I started to hang out with the girls. But one day when I went over there, one of their older brothers was there with a bunch of his friends, smoking a blunt in the bedroom. Everything was fine at first, but then all of a sudden they turned on the TV and put on this porno video of five guys gangbanging a girl. Before I knew what was happening, they all jumped on me and started pretending they were doing it. I was completely scared out of my mind. They acted like it was a joke, but I got this vibe in my feet and my stomach that told me to get out of there as fast as I could and never come back.

That was when I said, "Screw this, I'm going back to Marine City." I had a couple of friends there I knew I could stay with, so I packed my suitcase and told my mom I was leaving. She didn't argue with me. Of course she didn't want us there. And I didn't want her there, either! It was devastating for both of us. I wanted her to leave Detroit, leave that guy, get her own place and be normal again. But I knew she'd gotten trapped. She didn't have any money, she didn't have a car, she didn't have a job somewhere else. How was she going to leave? What was she going to do, couch-surf with me? She had nowhere to go, and she couldn't just pick up my little brother and go be homeless.

Tyler:

Cate and I had been together for three years when this was all going down. When she left Detroit, she came to my place first. My mom always had an open-door policy when our friends needed a safe place to stay. She's always taken care of my sister's friends when their parents kicked them out or whatever. But she has rules, and for Cate, the rule was that Cate could stay as long as she was going to school. Unfortunately, the school wouldn't let her enroll herself in the tenth grade without her mom there. Well, her mom was in Detroit without a car. So Cate didn't get to go to school. To this day that makes me furious. What's a kid in Cate's situation supposed to do when things go crazy at home?

So Cate and I had to lie to my mom and pretend she was going to school every day. She'd get up with me, leave the house like she was going to class, and come back to the house when my mom had left for work. Eventually, my mom found out. That was when she said, "Tyler, I can't do this. I have to call someone." She called up Cate's grandma in Florida, and Cate's grandma was like, "Hell, no. I'm not having my granddaughter bouncing around from couch to couch." So she called up Cate's mom and had custody temporarily signed over so that she could bring Cate down to stay with her in Florida until things had stabilized.

It all happened fast. I woke up one day and went to school like normal, and when I got home she was gone. There was a note on the counter that said, "I found out I was leaving and it was too hard to say goodbye. I love you so much." I was devastated. I bawled my eyes out for hours. She wrote to my mom, too, to thank her for everything she'd done, and when I got her on the phone we both cried. I wasn't mad at her, but I was mad. Three years together, and we were torn apart because these adults didn't have their shit together. First I was pissed at my mom, and then I was really mad at Cate's mom. I was like, "God, why would you let your daughter go to Florida?" Cate was left with no place to go just because her mom was with some stupid asshole in Detroit.

Catelynn:

I was in Florida for eight months and it was an extremely hard time. My grandparents are amazing, and they took great care of me. But it was a drastic change, and it all happened because my home life was messed up and out of control. There was nothing I could do about it. I was very angry, and very depressed. Not having anywhere to go or a stable place to live was devastating. I remember at that time in my life, I smoked marijuana as often as I possibly could. It was the only way I could think of to deal with my feelings and anxiety. If I wasn't high, I was so full of anger and helplessness I couldn't stand it. As long as I could find five bucks to get a joint, I didn't have to think about anything that was going on or what a nightmare my life had turned into.

Meanwhile, back in Detroit, my mom's boyfriend kicked up his crack addiction. The final straw was when he started pissing off the neighborhood drug dealers. One day my mom, my brother and her boyfriend were upstairs when someone knocked on the door. He went down to answer, and when my mom glanced out the window, she saw five guys standing outside on the street and two more on the porch. It was one of those old houses with a refurbished attic for the upstairs bedrooms, and there was a grate in the floor where you could see down into the living room. So she looked down through the grate as her boyfriend answered the door and let in one of the men outside, a guy he knew.

Her boyfriend always kept a baseball bat behind the door, just in case. This guy who came in grabbed the bat and smacked Dave in the head. As my mom watched, this guy got her boyfriend on his knees and held a gun to his head, saying "Give me the money you owe me, or I'll kill you right now." My mom screamed out that she was calling the cops. And this guy just shook his head and told her boyfriend, "I don't care about you, your woman, or your kids. I'll kill you right now."

Finally her boyfriend convinced the guy he'd get him his money, and the men left. That was it. My mom called my grandma and said, "I'm getting out of here." She moved back to her mom's house in Marine City. Their relationship wasn't good, but finally there was just no choice. After that, my mom found out that her boyfriend owed those guys something like forty-thousand dollars. He's still in Detroit now, living with two women and three kids.

When I finished the school year, my grandparents wanted me to stay in Florida and graduate there. They offered to get me a car if I got good grades, and everything. But I was young, and I just wanted to be home. I know that they knew it would be better for me to stay with them, but I could never understand why I wasn't able to go home. I didn't care that my mom was staying with her mom. I wanted my family, my friends, and Tyler. So I took off like a rocket as soon as I could.

My poor grandma. She tried to get me to go on birth control in Florida. I said, "No, thanks. Birth control would make me fat." She told me, "Pregnancy makes you fat, too." I laughed it off. And four or five months after I got back to Michigan, I was pregnant.

We Had to Do Different

Tyler:

Fast forward a few months, and here are my dad and Cate's mom trying to talk us into parenting the baby. With all that upheaval fresh in our minds. With Cate's mom just barely out of it and moved into a new trailer of her own. With my dad fresh out of prison. With the two of them drinking all night in the kitchen. Oh, and getting married.

And there we were, watching this whole thing unfold with a child growing inside of Catelynn. A child who didn't ask for any of this. A child we already loved enough to want the very best for.

It was so hard to be sixteen, scared, half-blinded by emotions, and hearing constantly from our parents that we were making a huge mistake and ruining our lives. We wanted their guidance. We wanted their advice and their support. It was hard as hell to have them condemn our decision.

But it was even harder to imagine bringing an innocent child into all that chaos and telling ourselves we'd done the right thing. And that was why the harder they fought us, the more we stuck to our decision. That was even truer once we started the adoption process and got to know the amazing couple we chose to adopt our baby. Every possible sign in the universe told us we were doing the right thing by doing different.

Catelynn:

Of course, it's easier to explain all this in retrospect. It really was chaos at the time. Sometimes we'd be lying in bed and we'd be like, how the hell did this happen to us? How are our parents married? How are we in this situation? We were in the middle of a tornado. We were just waiting for a piece of debris to fall on us.

It really wasn't until later that I started to fully understand the value of my decision, and the meaning of breaking the cycle. My dad's mom had him when she was sixteen. My dad had his son when he was sixteen. My mom's mom had her at sixteen. My mom had me at nineteen. And then I had Carly at seventeen.

They've all struggled their whole lives, paycheck to paycheck, and I was the only one who chose a different option. One night after it was all said and done, my dad's mom said to me, "Catelynn, I'm so proud of you for breaking the cycle." That was the first time I realized, "Wow, I kind of did."

Closing Thoughts

Adoption is not an easy decision, but sacrifice isn't supposed to be easy. Doing the right thing is usually harder than the wrong thing. And for most parents, the idea that the "right thing" means placing your child with another family goes against every natural instinct there is. For a mother who's dreamed of nurturing a child all her life, it's almost unimaginable at first. Maternal instinct can be one of the strongest forces there is. It's like that for almost every animal on the planet. Mother bears will kill to protect their cubs, but they don't drop them off with other bear families when their habitat gets destroyed. There's a real natural instinct separate from all logic and reason, and you can't mute that instinct with a list of pros and cons.

So we understand why some of our family members struggled with our decision. We struggled with it, too. But that's why at every step of the way, we had to remind ourselves to think of what was best for the baby. That child did not ask to be brought into this world. Children and babies are the most innocent, vulnerable, helpless creatures on the planet. They're relying on you for everything. Their lives will be defined by the choices made by the adults around them.

So we made this choice. We chose a better life for our child. That was the greatest expression of love we had to give.

CHAPTER 6:

THE ADOPTION JOURNEY

Now that we've talked for so long about the dark side of our sacrifice, it's time to let the bad memories rest for awhile. Let's not forget that this is a story of hope. And for every shadow along the way, there were beacons of light that supported and guided us down the path we believed in. Each of us had one parent who was against our decision, but each of us had another parent who had our backs for the long haul. Once we started down the road to adoption, we got to know more people who offered us the advice and reassurance we needed to navigate this unexpected and completely unfamiliar journey.

Yes, we were making a sacrifice. And yes, it was difficult. But as we were able to see through our own grief and frustration, we also saw the beauty and love that unfolded as a result of our choice. Because we chose adoption, and thanks to the guidance of our adoption counselor, we were able to make a life plan for our child that provided her with all the stability and opportunity we could dream of. At the same time, we were able to help grant a wonderful couple's biggest wish by giving them their first daughter.

We had already had a glimpse of adoption a year before when someone close to us had almost placed her child with an adoptive family. That was more of an education than most people in our position usually had. But experiencing it ourselves was another thing completely. Every stage was more intense than the next: Meeting the adoption counselor, searching for the perfect adoptive parents, checking into the hospital, and signing over custody over our parents' objections.

And in the middle of it all was a beautiful baby girl, completely innocent, surrounded by people who loved her enough to make sure she had the best chance she could have at an awesome life.

A Special Note on Positive Language

You may or may not have noticed that when we talk about adoption, we try to use positive language. Some of the most common expressions people use when they talk about adoption actually have some really negative connotations. Specifically, we ask that people take a minute to consider the meanings of the phrases "We gave our child up for adoption," or "We put our child up for adoption."

First of all, that phrase "give up" has a really negative feeling to it, doesn't it? When you "give something up," it sounds like you're either quitting, or letting go of something you've decided you don't need. It makes adoption sound like giving away a pair of shoes you don't have room for. Even just the words "give up" sound like the opposite of hope. For all those reasons, "You gave your child up for adoption," even though it's common, is something adoption educators discourage.

The terms "put up for adoption" sound nicer, but that expression actually has really dark origins. It goes back to the "orphan train" days of the eighteen-hundreds. Back then, missionaries would take poor children (not necessarily orphans) out of city slums and put them on trains headed West. The trains would stop at different cities and the children would be "put up" on the train platform. The locals would crowd around to see if there was a kid on the platform they wanted to adopt. The children who didn't get picked went on to the next stop. At best it was an early foster care system. At worst, it was a way for farmers in the West to pick up an extra worker. In any case, we try to do things better now.

Adoption has come a long way since then, even since just a few generations ago. Back in the 1950s, unexpected pregnancies were often handled in really shady ways. In many places, pregnant teenage girls would be shipped off to "boarding schools" where they'd finish out their pregnancy only to have their child whisked away from them, never to be seen again. That's why old-fashioned stories about adoption often involve a birth mom or adopted parent who have no way to find each other. But things have changed so much since then. Laws and regulations have been passed to legitimize adoption procedures and give everyone involved control over every step of the process. A parent who chooses to make an adoption plan has no reason to expect a scary, secretive experience that will leave them confused or helpless.

Things have changed. Modern adoption is a positive thing, so we try to stay away from the old negative language. Instead of saying "We gave our daughter up for adoption" or "We put our child up for adoption," we say "We placed our daughter for adoption" or "We made an adoption plan for our child." Using positive language reflects that adoption is a purposeful choice involving a careful plan for the benefit of the child.

It can be awkward to replace a phrase you're used to with a new one, but hopefully by the time you've read our story, you'll agree that the positive language is a way better fit for what adoption really means.

A First Preview of Adoption

Tyler:

When I was fifteen, my sister found out she was pregnant. She'd graduated from high school just three days before. It was not a happy surprise. She was a popular girl and a high achiever, and she had big plans to head for college and make something of her life. On top of that, she was no longer with the father, who had major anger issues. Nothing about the situation was ideal, to say the least. When she found out she was pregnant, she was freaking out.

She told my mom what was going on, and after my mom had her own freak-out, they started to discuss the options. In my sister's mind, there was no way she could take care of this baby; there was no chance the father would make a suitable parent, and besides, she had all of these plans for her life. So when my mom suggested making an adoption plan, my sister jumped for it immediately.

My mom helped her get the whole adoption set up. We drove down to Florida and met the couple who were hoping to adopt the baby. Everything was ready to go, right up to the day my sister gave birth.

Catelynn:

I was there at the hospital for the whole intense experience. The adoptive couple was there with the car seat and everything, ready to go. They fed Tyler's niece her first bottle, and they were all set to go home. We hung out with that family for three days. But Tyler's sister had struggled with her decision, and in the end, a new boyfriend talked her out of it in the hospital. It was devastating for the couple who had gotten all their hopes up. But it happens that way sometimes. Tyler's sister was a nineteen-year-old girl who'd just given birth and was recovering from her C-section, and she was vulnerable to those second thoughts. She just couldn't go through with it.

Tyler:

I remember the couple breaking down in tears. They were devastated. It was a tragic moment all around, but at the same time, I had my sister's back. Whenever she'd seemed indecisive, I was really worried about her being pressured one way or another. I was always telling people to back off. In the end she just didn't have enough peace with the adoption decision to resist this guy talking her out of it. She had to go with what she felt at that moment or risk regretting something forever. It was a rough moment, for sure.

Catelynn:

That entire experience was fresh in our minds when I got pregnant. We'd both had an up-close and personal look at adoption, and that was our main inspiration. When we realized we wanted to look into adoption for ourselves, Tyler's mom called and made an appointment for us just like she'd done for his sister. Soon enough we were sitting down with Dawn, our adoption counselor.

Looking at All the Options

Tyler:

One of the first things we discussed with Dawn was the different types of adoption we could go with. There are open, semi-open, and closed adoptions. Both open and semi-open adoptions involved contact between the birth parents and the child. The main difference between a semi-open adoption and a complete open adoption is that a semi-open adoption doesn't allow for face-to-face visits, while in an open adoption you actually get those physical meetings. A semi-open adoption involves photos and other kinds of communication, but not face-to-face contact.

Dawn told us the options, and at that first meeting, we looked at each other and said, "We definitely want it closed." We had our minds on a clean break in the beginning. We thought it would be better to have absolutely no involvement. We eventually started to soften up and thought we might have photos sent to my mom, and then my mom could hold onto them until we were ready.

Catelynn:

As we went back and forth on that part of the decision, I remember Dawn looking us in the eyes and saying, "You guys need to try and understand that this is going to be the hardest thing you've ever done in your life." We thought we got that, but we didn't. We couldn't. She did, though. And what she made sure to do was to make it clear that we were in complete control of the situation. She said, "You get to pick everything that you want for your child." Bethany Christian Services is very focused on what the birth parents want for the child. They'll do anything to help the birth parents.

Dawn even told us that we could go through the adoption agreements and add whatever we wanted in between the lines. She said we could do everything in pencil so we could erase it at any time if we started to feel uncertain or changed our minds about the terms. She thoroughly explained that we were in the driver's seat and we were the ones who would choose what happened with our child. The agency was extremely invested in the birth parents and what they want.

And if we changed our minds completely? That was all right, too. Dawn always told us: "There's nothing wrong if the day at the hospital comes and you decide this is not what you want after all. That wouldn't make you a bad person."

Tyler:

Of course, the adoptive parents have to be prepared for that possibility, too. Adoptive parents have to go through a lot. They have to take all these classes and go through a year of random visits from social workers who will stop by to see how things are. They have to write practically a whole book about their lifestyle, their family goals, the way they run their homes. They go through background checks and couples' therapy-type investigations to look at how they get along as a married couple. Because of all that, it's not unusual for adoptive parents to wait up to five years to get a child.

They also go through classes for grief and loss in case the birth parents change their minds, and they take classes about what the birth parents go through so that they can understand the thoughts and feelings on the other side. There are tons of counseling and therapy elements to help prepare them for the possibility that the adoption doesn't go through.

Catelynn:

During our talks with Dawn we came up with a list of things that we hoped to find in the adoptive family. We wanted them to have been together for a long time. We wanted them to be involved in their church. We were hoping to find a couple who were unable to have their own child, because we thought it would be such an amazing gift for them, and reinforced our idea that they would really cherish our child. We didn't want the couple to have any other kids because we wanted our daughter to be their first. We wanted the mom to be a stay-at-home mom. We had tons of points that we wanted.

Bethany Christian Services has a website where you can look at every single adoptive family that they have in every state. Tyler and I spent hours with his mom going through families in every state but Michigan — we thought having her in our own state would be too hard. We went through and read the entire biographies of these couples. Eventually I worked out a list of ten people I'd narrowed down, and I put stars next to the ones that I really liked. And the ones who really jumped out were Brandon and Teresa.

Reading Brandon and Teresa's biography, I just fell in love with them. They had been married for seven years, they'd traveled the world, they had college educations, and they were involved in their church. On paper, they were perfect. But what really cinched it was the video. They were the only couple on the list that had included a video in their biographies, and that gave us a chance to actually see the environment that our child could possibly grow up in.

In the video, Brandon and Teresa sat together on their porch and expressed their gratitude to the birth parents who had taken the time to look at their profiles. They explained how badly they'd yearned for a child, which they were unable to have on their own. It showed them at church, spending time with their family and friends, and people around them speaking to the camera about how much this couple deserved to have a child so much. I'll never forget this little boy in the video who prayed every night for Brandon and Teresa to get a baby from God. There was a friend on the video who had tragically lost a child, and explained how Brandon and Teresa had invested so much time and compassion into helping them through that horrible loss. There was obviously so much warmth and kindness between these people and in their world.

Tyler:

It was amazing, too, to see the actual house and the physical environment that they were hoping to bring a child into. We got to watch them moving around through the house, showing where the nursery would be for a boy, and what it would be for a girl, the living room, the kitchen. That was really reassuring.

When I got home that day to join Catelynn and my mom, she already had her top ten possible adoptive parents for us to go through. And she showed me the one with the video first. Once I saw it, I said, "I don't need to see anymore. That's them." She said, "We have nine more to look at!" And I said, "No. That's them. This is who we're supposed to have."

And we did. We just knew. Maybe it sounds weird. But we spent all this time going through all these hundreds of possible parents, so many of whom were obviously amazing people with wonderful homes. And when we found the right ones, it hit us in the chest like a ton of bricks. The rightness of the choice could not have been more obvious. When we knew, we knew. It was so weird. To be able to plan it out and find the people who fit everything we wanted for our kid was such an amazing experience.

Catelynn:

So we told Dawn that we found a couple that we liked, and she set up a meeting with them. We met with them at Bethany Christian Services, and we all sat down and talked about their jobs and their lives. We discussed how we wanted to send gifts and things, and talked about how open they wanted to be and we wanted to be. After we met at Bethany, we went to Starbucks and hung out for a few hours. We didn't look at anyone after that. We just knew these were the people we were going to go with. We had total peace with that decision.

Tyler:

I'll never forget the first moment we walked into the room to meet them. I went in first and said hello and shook hands, and Catelynn came in right after me. As soon as Teresa saw Catelynn, she just pulled her into a hug and held her tight for what seemed like fifteen minutes straight. They were totally silent. It was this magical, emotional, special moment. Teresa was hugging the woman who was carrying what could possibly be her child. And to see the love that she had for Catelynn, and to see her extend it so openly, was amazing. That connection was there. To us, and to our daughter.

Catelynn:

After that meeting, we just rolled forward. We never had a single moment of doubt that we had chosen the right parents for our child. I'm not even sure Brandon and Teresa knew what to make of the peace we had with our decision. I can remember many times during the pregnancy when we'd be talking to them on the phone and we could hear the nervousness on their end. They were so afraid to get their hopes up in case we backed out. They didn't want to get too close to us just in case. But I would always tell them, "You guys, don't be afraid. I'm not going to change my mind. You're going to go home with her. There's no reason to fear." I always tried to uplift them and make sure they knew. They probably thought I was crazy. They had gone through a loss before when birth parents had changed their minds, so they were on their guard.

Tyler:

There's a difference between the loss we feel placing our child, and the loss they risk of the birth parents backing out. As birth parents, we have control over the decision to hand the care of our child over to these parents we've vetted. And the sense of loss involved in that is huge, make no mistake. But the adoptive parents have a difficult experience, too. Especially considering the couples who are unable to conceive. It's very difficult for many people to come to terms with the fact that they can never have a biological child with the person they love, and that in itself can carry a lot of grief and sadness.

It was important for Catelynn and me to put ourselves in their shoes and understand where they were coming from. The whole adoption process, especially in an open adoption, is an ongoing experience.

We're still getting to know each other, still building and developing trust. It can get difficult at times. People are very sympathetic to us online. But fewer step back to think about what the adoptive parents go through. They have to put their entire family plan in some teenager's stomach, and that's an incredibly vulnerable thing for them. It's important to remember what they go through just as much as what the birth parents go through.

The Moment of Truth

Catelynn:

I think God knew what I was doing for Carly, so he decided to make the pregnancy easy for me. Besides morning sickness, I had back pain. But other than that, my pregnancy was awesome. I loved being pregnant with Carly. I wanted to keep her in there forever. It doesn't bother me at all! I could probably be a surrogate mother and just be pregnant all the time.

Giving birth was a little scarier, at least for a minute there. The idea of giving birth didn't seem totally real until I got to the hospital. Because we wanted everyone to be there at the same time, I had scheduled a day to be induced. The fear suddenly hit me when I put the hospital gown on. Then I thought, "Whoa, I don't want to do this at all." After carrying her for so long, the idea of not having her in there was terrifying to me. But you can't exactly turn around and run out the door. There was definitely no going back at that point.

Once we got started, I settled down. They induced me and broke my water and stuff, and the birth went smoothly, too. But, man, does that crap hurt. You can't even explain it. I'm not a pain person. I've never broken a bone or had any extreme pain (knock on wood), and I was not prepared for that. As soon as they offered me the epidural I was like, "YES! Give it to me!" After that I was fine. And once the whole thing is over, you don't feel anything. Some crazy hormone thing kicks in and you sort of forget the pain. Which is good, because otherwise, a lot of people probably wouldn't go back for seconds.

I was in labor for about four hours, pushed for eighteen minutes, and she was out. When I was pushing, I heard Tyler's mom going, "You're a baby-making machine, Cate! You're a baby-making machine!" Our daughter Carly was born at ten thirty-nine in the morning. Seven pounds, four ounces; twenty two inches long.

Tyler:

My mom was supportive of adoption the whole time, and so was Catelynn's grandma, her dad's mom, who flew from Florida to be with her for the birth. She had to skip her other granddaughter's graduation to come and be with Cate, which obviously meant a lot to us. Her dad wasn't able to be there, which was really hard on him, but he was there in spirit. And my mom and Cate's grandma were really the ones who stood by us. They were crying with us, holding us up and reminding us constantly that we were doing the right thing.

We had this whole plan. We told the doctors, "When she's born, take that baby and get her out of her as fast as you can." We were so afraid that listening to her voice and hearing her cry would be too much for us. We thought that natural parenting instinct would kick in. The plan was that after the baby was born, I'd cover her ears with my hands and put my forehead to hers to block her vision, and just talk to her as they took Carly down.

I said, "You're so strong, I love you so much, you're doing the right thing." But after Carly was born she was looking around asking, "Where is she? Where is she?" That just shows how strong those instincts are. She wanted to see her, she wanted to hear her, she wanted to know she was okay.

So we laid there for awhile, Catelynn took a shower, and I went down and looked at Carly and talked to Brandon and Teresa about how beautiful and perfect she was. Finally they wheeled her back into the room.

Catelynn:

We didn't change our mind about wanting an open adoption until the day Carly was born. Once she was born, it was real. We'd been scared that if we held her once, we'd never be able to let her go. But once we were able to spend time with her and share that time with Brandon and Teresa, we realized we were strong enough in our decision to allow that extra openness we had resisted. It was also obvious how hard it would be to not know where she was and what she was doing in life. That would make it ten times harder for us to heal. We still wanted to see them, see her, build a relationship with this family and be connected to the experience of her life. So we called Dawn over and said, "Break out the eraser. We want to change this agreement."

We stayed with her for three days straight, which is the usual maximum stay for women who have C-sections. I didn't have a C-section, but the doctors knew what we were doing and gave us the three days anyway. The hospital staff was really supportive, and the doctor and nurses came in every day to check on us. Brandon and Teresa had a room down the hall. For those three days we spent all our time talking to Carly, loving her, and taking pictures with her. We just soaked up as much as we could before we had to say goodbye.

Tyler:

We weren't the only ones who'd had doubts about how strong we'd be. There was this one older nurse who was very cold and standoffish to us, almost rude. She saw us spending all this bonding time with Carly in our room and she was convinced we weren't going to go through with it. She thought we were going to break this couple's heart. But she was the one who helped us out of the hospital, and she was crying her eyes out. When we got to the car, she gave Cate a hug and told her she was the strongest person she'd ever met.

It was a crazy intense hospital experience. It was emotional and intense and long and draining. And we still had one last blow coming to us when we went to sign over the legal rights to Carly's adoptive parents. Because guess who was there, objecting to our decision? My dad and Cate's mom.

Since Cate's mom refused to have anything to do with the adoption, Cate had to request a guardian for the day from the court system. And so there we stood, doing this incredibly difficult thing, and our parents were there on the opposite side of the courtroom. But the judge would barely give them the time of day. After they pleaded their case he looked at them and said, "I don't know what you're seeing in this situation, but I'm staring at these kids and watching them make the wisest decision of their lives. I'm denying your request to have any involvement in this, and if I were you, I'd wake up and realize these kids are doing an amazing thing."

Our parents stormed out of there, pissed off, and went speeding out of the parking lot. We were left there at the end of this traumatic experience watching them tear out of there in a rage. What more is there to say about that, except that it shouldn't have been that way?

Catelynn:

Since then, our parents have come around. They've apologized to us for not supporting us during that time, and we've forgiven them. And even though it still hurts to remember how unsupported we felt by them, I've found a way to channel that experience into helping others who are in the same situation. After my experience, I told Dawn that if a girl ever needed someone to talk to or support her, to give her my number. I wanted to make sure I was there to help, even if it was just by being someone these girls could talk to, someone who understood.

Since I gave birth to Carly, I've been a labor coach for several girls who just needed someone to be there with them when their parents weren't supportive and they need someone there, just to be there. And I always try and help them understand how much strength they have inside of them. I actually have a tattoo to remind me of the same thing every day: "You never know how strong you are until being strong is the only choice you have."

Tyler:

A lot of adopted children struggle with an identity crisis from not knowing who their parents were. But we made a scrapbook for Carly explaining our lives, our siblings, our favorite foods. Now we'll have this book and she'll have the show and she'll know exactly where she came from. That's the greatest blessing about doing the show and doing the adoption. She'll never have those questions. And she'll never doubt how much we've loved her and thought about her.

Part of the reason we decided to keep working with MTV was because we wanted all those adopted kids out there to see what their parents might have gone through, and how much love they put into their decision. For parents like us, it was the biggest act of love we could have done.

We want to be available to help people make the right decision. Not just to help the birth parents, but to help the children who are being brought into this world, through no choice of their own, and whose futures are at the mercy of adults' decisions.

Closing Thoughts

We've had many young people approach us with questions about adoption. And our response is always, "Look at your own life, think about all of the options, and choose the one that's right for you." We don't want to push anyone into anything.

We hear a lot of fear of adoption. People think they won't be strong enough to go through with it. To that we say, "You don't know how strong you are." We didn't think we were strong enough, but we followed what we knew was right, and in the end we were able to step up to what we believed in.

As for the people who still struggle with misconceptions about the adoption process and the motives of birth parents, we have two messages we want to spread. First, things have changed so much since the 1950s. Our adoption experience wasn't secretive or shameful. It was transparent and supportive, and we had control every step of the way.

Second, adoption is not an act of neglect or irresponsibility. The parent who chooses adoption is *choosing* to give their child a chance. That goes for the parents who choose closed adoptions and even the ones who make the choice and never look back. Even for them, adoption is an act of love. They didn't get an abortion. They didn't abandon the baby to neglect or worse. They made the conscious decision to put that child where there was a better chance of care and happiness.

The only point we really push is this: No matter what decision you go with, you're putting the child's needs and necessities before what you want. Because what you naturally want will almost always be to keep that baby. But that desire of yours doesn't always match up with what's best for the child. You have to keep that in mind. You have to always make sure that you're doing what's right for the person whose life is in your hands.

CHAPTER 7:

GROWING UP FAST

One of the weirdest misconceptions about adoption is that after the birth parents return home without the child in their arms, they shove the whole experience in the closet like a painful memory best forgotten. You see this play out in movies and stories about adoption all the time: An adopted kid grows up and tracks down his or her birth parents, and the parents act like a ghost has appeared on their doorstep. Like they haven't thought about that child in years. As if the birth parents' post-adoption experience is a matter of "out of sight, out of mind."

Nothing could be farther from the truth.

After the custody papers were signed and we watched Carly go home with another family, our lives didn't just bounce back to normal. How could anyone expect us to dive back into our crazy misbehaving teenager lives, drinking and smoking and partying? After all that we'd just been through, were we really supposed to just pick up where we left off like nothing had ever happened?

No way. No freaking way. We couldn't have done that if we'd wanted to. And the important thing was that we didn't want to at all. As Carly drove off with two wonderful parents, headed for the safe, secure and comfortable life we wished to God we would have been able to give her, we knew there was only one way to channel the storm of emotions raging inside of us. We were still just seventeen, but we sure didn't feel like it. From that moment on, we dedicated ourselves to becoming the kind of people our daughter would grow up to be proud of. It was time to turn our lives around.

When Nothing is the Same

Tyler:

Going back to life after Carly was really difficult. I remember being in Cate's room after it happened and just lying there, miserable, for hours. No matter how many positive things we can say about the decision to place our daughter for adoption, there's no getting around the grief and loss we experienced after we left without our daughter. Dawn had told us it was important to jump back into life as soon as possible. But that's a hard thing to do when that one thing that happened has changed everything in your life, and everything about you.

We did try. After we'd sat around depressed for awhile, I turned to Catelynn and said, "Let's go hang out. Let's see what Jeff's up to."

Cate started crying. "I can't," she said. When I asked why not, she said, "I can't just go out and have fun. I feel like I should be miserable, and distraught. I feel like I shouldn't be going out and having fun after what we just did for Carly."

I knew exactly what she meant. The goal was to get back into our lives and be normal, but it was so hard.

Catelynn:

After Carly was born, I stayed at Tyler's for about a week before I tried to go home. When I did, I got into a huge fight with Tyler's dad and my mom about the adoption. We weren't even close to making peace on that front. So I left again that night and went back to Tyler's. I stayed at his place for awhile. Him and his mom were my main support system at the time.

I never had any regrets or second thoughts. I knew where Carly was and I had peace with it, and I was comforted by the fact that we'd made things open, so it wasn't like I'd never see her again. But it was still incredibly painful.

You have to go through that phase of grief and loss. Your mind is racing. They say that in a strange way, even though you know your child is safe and sound, your feelings are similar to what you would go through if she had died. She was there in my arms, and then she wasn't, and I couldn't go and get her. I had just given birth to her, and all the mom parts of me were active. But she wasn't there. I couldn't see her. I couldn't check on her. I couldn't hear her. It was an enormous loss to deal with.

And on top of it there was that sense of, "I shouldn't be happy." Whether it was to punish myself or to try or because I just didn't know how to express the right emotions for this serious loss, I don't know. But I had this strong feeling that I should stay at home, be sad and not do anything for a couple of months. In reality, yes, you're supposed to go out and do things and have fun. Every counselor gives you that advice. But it's very difficult for a birth parent to do at first. It took at least a couple of months to get back into the groove.

Tyler:

We knew it was important to try to follow the advice and get ourselves out there. So we dragged ourselves out of the house, met up with our friends, had a good time and everything. But it wasn't the same as before. We couldn't just go out and start drinking and doing drugs. It was impossible. We were so impacted by this long, drawn-out experience that everything felt different to us.

After a couple of weeks we finally talked about it with each other. Cate said, "Isn't it weird how when we hang out with certain friends, we don't laugh at their jokes anymore? Have you noticed that?"

"Yes!" I said. "Totally!" We had this whole conversation about all of these weird changes we felt had happened. There were so many differences between our lives before and after Carly that we never could have imagined. Things we thought were funny before just weren't anymore.

Things that used to be fun before didn't interest us now. Our friends would invite us out to a party, and we'd look at each other and have this awkward realization that we'd rather just go home and watch movies.

Things changed for us. Our desires and ideals were different. Once we realized that, we had to figure out how to mesh our new outlook on life with the friends who hadn't experienced this life-changing ordeal that we'd experienced. People thought once we'd chosen adoption we'd dive back in like, "Cool! Time to go back to getting wasted." That's not what happens. Your brain doesn't let it happen. So we had to make compromises like, "We're not going to go party all night, but we'll hang out for a bit."

Then we'd go home and watch movies and be like, "What's wrong with us? Are we seventeen years old or fifty?"

Catelynn:

When you go through such an adult experience, it forces you to grow up. Dealing with the pregnancy and making an adoption plan put us in a very grown-up position, and after so many months in that position, we got used to looking at the world in a more grown-up way. It was just all of the thinking, all of the hard decisions, all the sacrifices. We really became like adults in those nine months. We realized how life works. Stuff is real. Serious things happen.

Not only did we have a more realistic and mature understanding of the way life worked, but we had a new understanding of its meaning and purpose. Doing what we did for Carly made us appreciate the makings of our own lives more. It made us realize that we needed to do something more with ourselves. We weren't going to just place our child in adoption and then go back and go on being losers, doing drugs and flunking out of school. That was out of the question.

Placing Carly wasn't just a gift, it was a promise. And that promise was, "We're going to become the kind of people who deserve to be parents." We were going to make our lives ten times better than what they were, so that when we were ready to have another child, we'd be in the position to say "This child will be safe, secure, and happy in our home."

Of course, we had to figure out how to make that happen. Before Carly, I had no real goals or dreams other than being a mom and a wife someday. Now I knew that I needed to see drastic changes in my life to make that come true. But we didn't have a roadmap or anything. So we sat down and started making a plan for ourselves.

Tyler:

We were still reeling with our grief and loss, but we started trying to turn our pain into motivation. It was like, "We feel this pain, but we're not going to feel it for nothing." Instead of letting it drag us down, we channeled it into this mission of turning our lives around.

The first thing was to set our goals. Before Carly, my main goal in life was to not get suspended. I knew I needed to aim a little higher than that if I wanted to make something of my life. So we sat down and thought, "What do we need to do?" For our ultimate goal, we wanted to get our lives to the point where if Catelynn got pregnant again, we would be ready and qualified to be parents. That meant we had to overcome all those "cons" in our lives that made us decide to place Carly in adoption. What did we have to do to make ourselves ready to be parents?

Honestly, a big part of our plan was just turning into normal people. A lot of that might sound simple to others: Graduating high school. Getting a job. Getting a cell phone. Getting a car. Going to college. But coming from our backgrounds, all of those goals would be major achievements. And they were all benchmarks we definitely had to hit before we could consider ourselves ready for a child.

Catelynn:

The first main goal was graduating high school. Before Carly, I just didn't care about my education. I didn't plan on going to college or have any idea what I wanted to do with my life. But as soon as she was born, I said, "I'm going to graduate high school, go to college, and do things that will benefit society. I'm not going to be some loser who's high on drugs and fighting." That was it. Tyler and I just sort of looked at each other and said, "Time to pull our pants up and get this done."

I had failed all of middle school, and we both messed up ninth grade. Then, obviously, we were dealing with the pregnancy and adoption. But we were able to turn things around by going to an alternative school called Riverview, which was amazing for us. We were a little behind schedule — Tyler was three months late, and I was a year late — but we stuck to it and graduated with our diplomas.

We didn't have to stop hanging out with our friends or anything. We still liked them and we knew they hadn't gone through what we'd been through. We'd go out and do bonfires and have a good time, but it just wasn't as much. After Carly, we'd do all the same things but in a different way. We'd have a beer and enjoy the company, but we wouldn't get smashed and pass out. We stopped being the last people at the party and started going home at twelve thirty.

Time to Get to Work

Tyler:

My very first job was at a pizza shop, running deliveries. I was excited about it at first! But my boss was a pizza nazi. He was in the military for five years, and he got it in his head that the place had to be run like a military base. There were all these things we had to do: When we clocked in, we had to scream "DRIVER IN!" And when we left, "DRIVER OUT!" He'd scream, "PEPPERONI!" and I'd have to scream back, "ROGER! PEPPERONI!" Dude, it's not war. It's pizza!

Everyone who worked there was miserable. I kept asking the other guys, "How do you put up with this for this long?"

"It's not that bad," they all said. "You just learn to listen and keep your mouth shut." Well, assuming you didn't skip the first half of this book, you can probably guess where this is going.

The Pizza Nazi had one of his sons working there, and the kid was, well, a little awkward. We didn't talk much. But one day when I was folding boxes I asked him, "So you must get paid pretty well working for your dad, right?"

"Oh," he said. "I don't get paid."

"Dude!" I exclaimed. "What are you doing here, then?"

"I don't know. This is just what I do." Turned out this kid went home every day from school, dropped off his backpack, and came to slave away for the Pizza Nazi for nothing.

"That's bullshit!" I was outraged. "You're working full-time for free! I can't believe this. He has to pay you. You need to stick up for yourself!"

The kid got all nervous and told me to lower my voice. He wasn't ready to take a stand, that was for sure. But that was one more reason for me to narrow my eyes at the Pizza Nazi every time he walked by.

The last straw was this stupid test he used to secretly trick all the drivers into. We all used GPS on our phones to deliver the pizzas, which was the obvious, simple way to do it. But the Pizza Nazi had a buddy whose house was in a really weird spot that always confused the GPS. If you didn't write down the exact directions, your phone would send you somewhere crazy. The Pizza Nazi knew this, but he wouldn't say anything about it. In his mind, it was a test to see how long it would take us to realize something was wrong with the route and how fast we'd call him to ask for help.

Of course I wasn't about to call the Pizza Nazi unless it was my last resort. When I realized I was lost, I thought I could figure it out. But then my phone died, and I had to admit defeat. I turned around and stopped at a little fabric store and used their phone to call Fort Pizza. I came clean and said, "I couldn't find the house and my phone and GPS died. I'm on my way back. What should I do? Do you have the customer's number so I can call them?"

"Get your ass back here!"

When I got back, the Pizza Nazi went off. He talked a tough talk and told me this was the last strike. I said, "You know what, dude? You're absolutely right." I took my hat off, tossed him my apron with a big smile, saluted everyone and got the hell out of the Pizza Nazi's dungeon.

That was when I realized I wasn't really good with overbearing bosses. I went and got a stockroom job for a retail company where Catelynn worked. That went much better.

Catelynn:

In retail you definitely have to deal with dicks. But I'm good under pressure. I'll just smile and say, "Okay, thank you, have a nice day!" Then I turn around and bitch about whatever happened. That job was pretty easygoing, and it was nice to have Tyler working in the back. Sometimes we'd be able to take lunches together.

But pretty soon we both found something we liked a lot better. Tyler's sister had worked for this company that placed caregivers for people with special needs, and we thought that would be a really valuable job for us to take on. We filled out applications and took all the necessary first aid and CPR classes, and then they filled out our profiles and matched us with people. I worked with a twenty-one year old girl with Down's Syndrome, and Tyler worked with a twenty-four year old guy with autism.

We loved the job, although it was incredibly draining. You have to have really high energy and be really excited all the time. There's a lot of burnout. In our case it was Monday through Friday, two-thirty to seven, with no breaks at all. You're at their homes, eating your meals with them and being at their side all the time. The agency gave us information about what our people needed to work on, so there were lots of goals and checkpoints to work toward. I was trying to help my girl become as independent as possible. I would coach her through taking a shower, blow-drying her hair, cooking for herself, and all the other little tasks most people take for granted.

It was exhausting sometimes, but so rewarding! The best part was when they learned something for the first time and you could see the progress they were making. What always bugged me was when I'd go home for the weekend, then come back on Monday to see that she'd lost all of her progress because her parents weren't keeping up the routine we'd planned to instill all of the things that I was helping her build up. Still, I would do that job again in a heartbeat, as long as it was one-on-one or with parents who were committed to the program.

Tyler:

The guy I worked with was much more independent. He lived on his own already, in a house his parents had gotten for him. He was autistic, but he was very capable. His parents had treated him just like their other kids and tried to raise him to be as independent as possible. They liked me as his caregiver because I promised never to do anything for him without giving him a chance to do it himself. When this kid would say, "Tyler, make me pancakes!" I would say, "Nope. You make your pancakes. When I'm not here, you make your own pancakes. When I'm at home, I make my own pancakes. So you make your own pancakes."

And he was down with that! At least, most of the time. I did have to hold my ground during some tantrums, and that wasn't easy at all. He was a huge guy about six-foot-three and two-hundred pounds, and when he got mad he'd smack his head and stomp on the ground. It was freaky for me because he could totally destroy me. But I had to hold steady and make sure he knew I was standing firm. It was a good experience for me to actually experience the authority side of things for once and see how I handled it. It wasn't too bad at all!

You Can't Fix Everything

Catelynn:

While we were working hard to get our lives to a different place, we still had the same old environments to deal with. After enough time had passed, my mom and Tyler's dad finally started to come to terms with our decision. My mom felt horrible about fighting with me during all that, and she apologized to me in tears. We were able to make peace on that specific issue. But there was a lot more going on that was hard to deal with.

My mom and Tyler's dad stayed married for six years, and in that time they brought out all the worst in each other. They were so comfortable with each other's bad habits there was really nothing to hold them back. After Carly was born and they moved into a different house, things got a lot worse than we even knew. They wouldn't do things in front of us, but we found out later about the stuff that was going on in that house. They'd drink all night, or take pills, or even smoke crack together.

Tyler:

They were both addicts. And they sheltered each other from shame and judgment. They got comfortable with it. And then whatever problems they didn't already have in common, they started sharing with each other. For example, Cate's mom wasn't into crack, and my dad never smoked it at home. That's the thing with addicts. They can't follow the rules you need them to follow, but they're not soulless. They still have their own moral codes they hold onto as hard as they can. And for my dad, that was always his one single rule as an addict: No smoking in the house. That's why he would leave on crack binges for three days at a time and come back when he was done. During those benders, we'd all be calling the jails and hospitals trying to keep track of him and make sure he was still alive. That was the reason my mom left him back in the day.

But with Cate's mom, the issue was that she didn't want to be alone. She hated being left there by herself while he went off and did his thing. She'd beg him to just stay there with her, whatever it took. But for him it was a choice between staying home, crack-free, or going out and smoking crack. He always chose the crack. Finally Cate's mom got so desperate to keep him there she said, "Screw it. I don't want you to leave. Get the drugs, come back, and smoke them here so you're not out there leaving me by myself."

That's how it all escalated. Once he was doing it there in front of her, it wasn't long before she was doing it with him. It was a bad line to cross for both of them. My dad even told me that was the first time he'd broken his one rule. Twenty years he'd been doing it, and he'd never smoked it at home in front of the kids. And as soon as he did, guess what? Cate caught him.

Catelynn:

He was in the bedroom smoking it when I walked in. I completely freaked out. I went absolutely crazy. I was yelling at him, demanding to know how he could do that with kids in the house, calling him a piece of shit. I was so shocked and upset and furious. I could tell how high he was by the look in his eyes. And I could tell he was caught off guard and ashamed, because normally he'd freak out at me for yelling at him. But this time he was stuttering and refusing to look me in the eye.

I called Tyler crying my eyes out. I told him what had happened and that I didn't want to be in that house anymore. Not a week later, I moved in with him. I just felt more comfortable at Tyler's house. It was a safe place for me where I could feel comfortable and normal. His mom was there, and he was there. There was just no comparison.

Tyler:

I was shocked when she told me he was smoking crack in the house. I thought, "Damn, he's really going off the rails if he broke that rule." He told me later he'd never been so ashamed in his entire life, that he couldn't even look at Catelynn after she'd seen him doing that.

My dad and Cate's mom were married for six years, but they only really spent six months together. The rest of the time, he was in jail. He was constantly in and out of jail because their relationship was so messed up they got hit with a no contact order, which they then kept ignoring.

The no contact order was sparked by a fight they had in Richmond, which ended with the cops coming and taking my dad to jail for the first domestic case he had ever had brought against him. In Michigan, the state pursues domestic violence cases no matter what. Once Cate's mom realized what the no contact order meant, she tried to write the parole board to lift it. But they told her it wasn't going to happen, one of the reasons being that he never completes his parole.

So the no contact order remained in place. And they kept breaking it. And he kept going back to jail. The chaos continued, the same way it always did for them individually, and the same way they were comfortable with it together. That was what they were used to, and they just weren't about to get out of that cycle.

The Kindness of Strangers

Tyler:

Some of what we've talked about in the last couple of chapters might be familiar to you if you know us from MTV. Our involvement with the show became an important factor in the direction we decided to take our lives. Not because of the cameras or the media attention, but because it opened us up to the love and support of the many, many amazing people who reached out to us after watching our story unfold.

Cate and I were featured on MTV's reality TV series *16 & Pregnant*, which documented the pregnancy, the adoption, and our experiences after placing Carly. Like all of the other teen parents featured on *16 & Pregnant*, we had no idea what a huge deal it was going to be or that we'd be asked to return for another series following our lives. The show brought on a lot of attention from the press, and tons of reactions from viewers. That turned out to influence us in huge ways.

Catelynn:

This was back in the days of MySpace. After *16 & Pregnant* aired, we started getting all of these messages on MySpace. For days and days we were just swarmed with messages. And not just little messages like, "Hey, what's up," but thoughtful, personal messages that were pages long. And almost every single one of them was positive.

For days and days we were just shocked by this huge outpouring of love and support from all of these strangers. It was message after message from people of all ages, telling us how we'd inspired them. People were sharing their life stories, thanking us for our strength and honesty, encouraging us to hold our heads up and stay strong.

It was insane to realize that just from that one hour on TV, people felt connected to us and were willing to share their life stories. Not only that, but to extend so much kindness and support to us. And it could not have come at a more important time. In a way, the people who supported us from day one really helped us through our grief and loss.

Tyler:

When the show aired, we were still deep in our grief and loss. We were waking up every day depressed because we didn't have our daughter with us. All of that love and support gave us a boost during our darkest times. On the days when we were really down, we'd go online and read all of these messages of positivity and support. It uplifted us so much to know that all these people were rooting for us. And it showed us that just by sharing our story, we'd already taken a step toward making something meaningful out of our lives.

Once we shared our adoption story and started to see the impact it had on such a huge number of people, we started to think about how many people have been somehow affected by adoption. Adoption is a big part of a lot of families, whether it's touched the life of an immediate or distant family member, a parent or a sister or an uncle or a cousin. But the weird thing is that it's still not something that we discuss in an educational, accurate way. There are still a lot of misconceptions out there about adoption. Even though the process of adoption has evolved, the conversation hasn't. It still is sort of quiet and hush-hush.

Catelynn:

So many of the responses we got came from adoptive parents and birth parents who had placed children in adoption. They wrote things like, "I've been waiting and waiting for someone to get it right. Thank you for showing this process the way it really happens." When we thought about it, we realized they were right. Birth parents are misinterpreted in the media all the time. Maybe you've seen one of those crazy old made-for-TV movies where some deadbeat birth mom shows up to tear a family apart, and she's hiding in bushes and stalking the kid, or whatever. Or you've seen some sad story about a kid who finds out she was adopted and tracks down her birth parents only to get the cold shoulder. There are lots of dramatic and tragic stories about adoption that play out in the media. But there aren't a lot of places where you can find birth parents represented accurately or positively. We didn't realize it when we agreed to do the show, but our representation of adoption was something that was really rare and really needed by a lot of people.

Tyler:

The real kicker was when we got a letter from a girl who told us that we'd inspired her to make her own adoption plan. She told us it was thanks to our story that she found the strength and peace to take that step and place her child for adoption. After that, we realized we had the chance to really make a positive impact on people. Before that, we weren't sure if we wanted to keep showing our lives on TV. It was kind of like, "What are we doing here, really?" But when we thought about that letter and the fact that we had actually helped inspire someone to do something so important, we decided we had to keep going. And we swore as long as we did, we'd be as open, honest, real and raw as we could. We figured authenticity was what had helped us connect with people, and after that, connecting with people was what we wanted to do.

Closing Thoughts

The day we sent Carly home with her adoptive parents was the day we realized that our lives would never be the same again. Things that we used to find fun, like partying with our friends, were no longer going to cut it. There was no going back. Hell, we wouldn't have even wanted to. We may have still been two teenagers in high school, but at that point we felt like fully grown adults and we were ready to take on new responsibilities.

Seeing our lives from a new perspective, and with Carly on our minds every single day, we were motivated to become the type of birth parents that Carly would be proud of one day. We were motivated. Not only would having jobs give us a little bit of financial independence but we wound up doing something extremely meaningful.

At the pizza joint Tyler quickly learned the qualities he did not want in an employer. He also learned a lot about himself and how he deals with certain situations in the workplace. Growing up, Tyler had been responsible for himself and his mom had always respectfully laid down the law when it came to chores. When his boss would bark orders and treat him like a child, well, that didn't sit well with him. Disrespect from authority figures just wasn't going to fly. We both did well working at Rue 21, so at least it wasn't a problem everywhere! But still, we wanted more than food service and retail, and working with people with special needs was the perfect next step. It felt good to use our new independence to teach others how to be independent themselves. On an important personal level, it helped us channel our parental instincts into something that felt positive instead of painful. And best of all, it gave us the chance to make a difference in people's lives.

That meant more to us than anything. And it reaffirmed that we had made the right choice when it came to placing Carly in adoption. Would we have been able to take such quick steps toward becoming responsible, mature, financially stable adults if we had been scrambling to make ends meet for a baby? Our upbringings were a good indication that the answer was a big fat no. Because of our choice we had the opportunity to take control of our futures and make a difference in people's lives. In our mission to make Carly proud, we found real reasons to be proud of each other...and proud of ourselves.

While we focused on making strides off camera, we never expected the amount of love and support that was about to come our way from the time we spent on camera. We were completely taken by surprise when MTV viewers responded to our story with an outpour of love and support. And we were shocked when we realized how many lives it had touched. We never knew how badly people needed a positive adoption story like ours on a mainstream level. It quickly became clear to us that our purpose in life was to show these people they weren't alone. There was no longer a reason for us to question our roles on MTV. If we could make a difference in people's lives and make a positive impact on people, we were going to do it.

CHAPTER 8:

HOLDING ONTO EACH OTHER

Crisis can bring a couple together. But oftentimes when the dust settles, you look around and realize the landscape has completely changed. You're older now, and you've changed in ways you don't yet understand. In our case, we went from a fairy tale childhood romance to an experience that pushed us even closer and left us with a bond — a child — that would stay between us forever. And once we got through the struggle, the heartbreak and the aftermath, we found ourselves passing into the next phase of our life together.

So, what then? Well, for years we had been the ideal couple: never fighting, always a team. But the reality was that we each still carried our own issues that were just waiting to pop up and cause some mayhem. Our effort to grow up and be serious about our lives was like renovating a house from top to bottom: You're bound to stumble on rotten beams and structural weakness you never suspected. And that's exactly what happened to us.

But what do you do? Burn down the house? Hell, no! You put your heads together, call a contractor — or a relationship counselor — and do what you have to do to make that house stronger than ever.

First Real Test

Catelynn:

Stress never came between Tyler and me. If anything, it brought us together. We united and supported each other during the hardest times, and we never treat our relationship as a place to dump negativity or take out our frustrations on each other. Obviously we're not sweet and cuddly with each other all the time. There are times when one of us is in a bad mood and starts acting kind of short or snippy. But the good thing about being open and honest is that if one of us notices that change, they'll just ask. Basically, if one of us is mad about something specific, we come out and say it. So if I notice Tyler being a little rude and I don't know why, I'll just ask, "Are you crabby?" And he'll say, "Yeah, I'm crabby." Then I'll say, "Can I ask why?" And either he'll tell me what's going on, or he'll tell me he doesn't want to talk and I'll leave him alone. There are times when we snap at each other, obviously. But we don't let it escalate, and we always say we're sorry we know we've acted out. It's easier to own up to being a jerk than to blame it on the other person.

Tyler:

When we say a relationship is hard work, we don't mean to make anyone think it's not worth it. It really is just like taking care of a house. There are chores you have to do, and sometimes stuff gets broken, and you have to fix it. Those parts aren't fun or easy, but they're necessary to keep things in working order.

Actually, chores are a great example. When we first moved in together, we realized we both hated doing the dishes. So for awhile they'd pile up while each of us put it off, and then whoever caved and did them would be really annoyed about it. Then we came up with a life-changing solution. Instead of letting the dishes pile up, we wash them as soon as we're done. If you're at the sink putting a dish in there, you can take five extra seconds to wash it. And if one of us forgets, like if I go to wash my glass and I see one of Cate's dirty plates in the sink, we don't make a huge deal out of it. I just say, "Babe, you left your plate in the sink." She says sorry. I say it's okay, and I wash it. There. Done. Nobody gets stuck dealing with a huge pile of dishes.

That's exactly how we try to handle our relationship. When a "dirty dish" or a problem is there, we clean it. No pile-ups allowed. But, hey. We're not perfect. I'm not perfect. Cate's not perfect. These things are easier said than done. And sometimes a dirty dish just comes flying at your head.

Catelynn:

Our first major challenge as a couple traced back to those eight months I spent in Florida, and a problem I'd had for my entire life: Lying. Tyler and I got really good about being honest with our feelings in our relationship, and it made us really strong. But for me, personally, lying had always been an issue. For my whole life, I had a habit of telling people what I thought they wanted to hear, even if it wasn't the truth.

I didn't grow up with Tyler's obsession with the truth. I watched my mom lie all the time. To her boyfriends, to me, whatever. And I got used to lying to her, or to them, about whatever it was easy to lie about. If the truth was going to start a conflict, I was not going to tell the truth.

But even if the habit originally came out of a fear of conflict, it's not good to get used to messing with the truth. Lots of my lies came with a feeling that I was protecting other people. I thought if I told them what they wanted to hear, it was better for everyone. But now I know that lying doesn't really protect anyone but yourself. And what I learned the hard way was that lies always come out, eventually, and once the truth has been twisted into a lie, it's way harder to deal with. Not many things can do as much damage to a relationship as a lie.

Once a Liar, Always a Liar?

Tyler:

Lying was what sparked our first major fallout as a couple. It stemmed back to those eight months in Florida, where it turned out she secretly dated another guy. Two years later, after I found out, it was the closest I've ever been to walking away from our relationship. All of our relationship coping skills couldn't hold a candle to this conflict. We had to work through some serious, serious issues to get through it.

I spent that whole year waiting for Cate. We talked every single day on the phone for two hours at a time. If we didn't talk to each other one day, we'd freak out. We talked for two hours and kept in touch. We told each other "I love you, I can't wait to see you," all of that. I was going to an alternative school, and one day in science we got to make our own sterling silver rings. So I literally hand-made a ring for Catelynn, carved our anniversary date, and kept it to give to her when she got home. I even tried to go down to Florida to see her, but there just wasn't money in my world for that. One of our friends was able to go, and I was so jealous I was furious.

I knew Florida was a different kind of experience for Catelynn. She wasn't there by choice. She was basically forced to live there because the only place in Michigan she could call home was a drug house in the Detroit ghetto. I knew it was a complicated experience for her. But it was also her chance to have a fresh start. She got to change her clothes, she got to figure out what kind of person she wanted to be. It was a special kind of escape for her.

When she came back to visit for Christmas, she spent the whole vacation at my house. I remember thinking she was so different. She was styling her hair, putting a lot of makeup on, and she had all this confidence I couldn't remember. She would put her hand on her hip and pose for pictures like she'd never done before. Of course I got really excited about it, and then she had to go to Florida.

Catelynn:

Florida was a huge, drastic change for me. I was so used to being able to do what I wanted and not have to answer to anyone. But my grandparents were very strict. Severely strict! And I wasn't used to that. I wasn't used to discipline. At my mom's, I could always come and go as I pleased and run all over town. But there, it was way different.

So I suddenly caught myself rebelling a lot. I started sneaking out to hang out with friends I made there. After my grandparents caught me sneaking back in a couple of times, they took my door off the hinges as punishment. They were not putting up with that trailer park wild-child stuff at all. Eventually I got better and settled down, but I was still going through a lot of anger and anxiety, and I was always looking for ways to get my mind off of it. Like I said earlier, at that time I was basically addicted to marijuana. I know you can't technically get addicted to marijuana, but there's nothing else you could call it. I had to be high all the time.

That was where this Florida guy came in. He was this older guy who was chill and always had weed and cigarettes. I was always willing to hang out and smoke weed, and one thing led to another. It didn't take a psychic to predict where that was going.

Tyler:

During those eight months when Cate got her other boyfriend, and I was just in Michigan waiting. Our agreement was that we were going to wait for each other, but at that age, how long are you really going to do that for? Obviously she didn't leave me. We still talked every single day. But that's almost what made it so bad. She was lying to me that whole time. I'd call and ask what she was doing and she'd say she was with her friends. Then I'd hear a rustling around and I'd hear her say "Shh," and suddenly the phone would hang up. Later I found out every time I called she was at her boyfriend's house, and she had to go outside to the porch to talk to me. He'd come out and ask her a question or something, and she'd have to hang up real quick.

Once I found out, I was hurt. But then I thought about it so much that I got into this weird obsessive state. I wanted to know every detail about him. What was his name? How tall was he? What color was his hair? And the details I heard just made me more fixated: He was eighteen years old, he had a job, a sports car, he lived in his own place. I started comparing myself to him, everything he had against everything I didn't. It just killed me to think about it. I got obsessed with every single detail. Especially the sex.

The thing was, this brought out a lot of my own issues, too. First of all, my obsession with the truth. My whole thing wasn't really that she had this boyfriend, it was that she didn't tell me about it. Of course we had an agreement to wait for each other, but we weren't stupid. We knew that was a hard thing to stick to at our age. I felt like she could have come clean with me and we could have gone from there. Instead I felt like I was played for the whole eight months. The lying was what got me! The girl I'd been with before Cate had lied to me all the time, and I swore I'd never go through that again. And that's where my stubbornness kicked in, because once I've made a vow to myself, I start seeing things in black and white. And that can make things even worse.

But also there was this fixation I had on sex. I could not stop thinking about the sex. The movie in my head was just them having sex. My stomach would turn, I'd feel nauseated. It literally made me sick to my stomach. And I thought if I asked her everything and got the dirty nitty gritty nasty details, I could make the movie go away. I got so obsessed with every detail. I went into so much. I asked how many times they had sex, what did they do, did she like it, all of this, all of that.

Catelynn:

When we were going through that, I was terrified. I couldn't believe I was going to lose something I really wanted because of something so stupid. The fact was, I hated who I was in Florida. I had dated this guy because he bought me cigarettes and weed. He was helping me to rebel. I was using him to get things I wanted. I just don't like to think about it. If I could go back in time, I would take all of that back.

In Florida I went from being this prude girl who had so much respect for myself, to being the type of girl who would date a guy basically because he always had weed and cigarettes. That made me feel horrible about myself. I felt like a slut, honestly, and that was something I never wanted to be.

And once I was back home with Tyler, I just wanted to leave the whole memory behind. A big part of the lie was that I was so obsessed with wanting to protect Tyler's feelings, and our relationship, that I just didn't want to tell him something that would be so bad. But part of it was also that it was a really bad memory for me, something I hated to think about. After it came out I used to cry to him and say, "I hated the person I was when I lived there, and I won't ever go back to that."

Tyler:

I had to fight against my own stubbornness to even try and work it through. It wasn't even my brain and my heart saying different things. Part of my brain was telling me to stick with my guns, that if she'd lied to me about this she'd lie to me again. But another part of my brain was telling me to cool it for a minute. I had to force myself to think about whether this was really unfixable, whether it was really worth giving up the relationship.

So we tried to give it a shot. And from my end, what was feeding the issue was my obsession with knowing every detail. I was so psycho that I demanded this guy's number so I could call him and get all the details she didn't want to share with me. So she gave me his number, and I sent him a text pretending I was Catelynn. I said, "My boyfriend's probably going to get in contact with you. He asked me for your number so just tell him what happened and be honest with him."

This guy wrote back, "Why? Okay, whatever." And then, still thinking he was texting Catelynn, he wrote, "Do you want me to tell him we talked last night on the phone?" That made me stop cold. I got in touch with Cate and asked her when she'd talked to her boyfriend in Florida. And she said, "I haven't talked to him in five months."

"That's it," I said. "You're busted. I caught you. You're done." We broke up for three weeks. I thought that was the end of it.

Catelynn:

There's no way to explain how helpless and terrified I was during that whole thing. All I could think about was how I might lose the best thing in my life based on this one stupid thing that I knew, one-hundred percent knew, that I would never do again. And the fact that it was really the lie that had him the most upset was even harder to deal with. Because lies really had become normal for me, even if I had learned to be honest, too. Lying was definitely a habit I fell into frequently, and I hadn't experienced the damage it could cause before that. It was a devastating wake-up call.

United We Conquer

Tyler:

I'm really headstrong. I don't know if I've mentioned that. But I was stubborn on this, too. Cate tried to talk to me the whole three weeks, and I forced myself not to. But deep down I really wanted to just let the whole thing go because I loved her so much. My heart was battling with my stubbornness.

In my head I was thinking, "Tyler, just leave her. She lies once, she'll lie again." But in the end I thought, "She's too good to let go for something like this."

I could see her coming face to face with this problem of lying that she'd never really confronted before. She was struggling to work through something inside herself the way we'd struggled through so many things together. And I thought, "I have to help her with this." I didn't want to break up and regret it over something we could have worked through together.

Eventually I texted her and suggested we go back to counseling. So I decided we should get some help and figure out why I was so creepily obsessed with this, and then figure out why Catelynn was lying and how to stop it.

And then it all came out in counseling why she lied and all of that. Lying is something you learn. She had to lie all her life to keep the peace. She learned about it from living in that house. It really came down to, "Can you live the rest of your life with her and get over this?"

Catelynn:

Going through counseling was actually very beneficial. Not only did I learn why I was lying to him, but I learned why I lied, period. It was because I was always trying to protect people around me. It was a huge awakening for me. And it was like, "Really, Catelynn, do you want to go on like this? Do you want to lose this person you loved and know you ruined something amazing over something so stupid?" No. I did not.

And ever since that, I've been a totally different person. I don't lie. I tell him what's up. I was willing to learn. I told him, and I meant, that I would do everything to make it better. It hurt me so much that I had hurt him. I would cry not because of myself but because of what I had done to him and the pain I had caused him. If I could go back, I never would have done any of that.

Tyler:

In counseling we talked about my psychotic obsession with the sex that was involved. Most couples say it's the emotional side of cheating that matters the most, like the important thing is whether or not it "meant anything." But I felt like I would have been fine if they were madly in love. I was obsessed with that specific physical part of the relationship. I was worried about the sexual things. I don't think I ever asked if she loved the guy. I didn't give a shit. I wanted to know all about the sex. That's weird. It was weird, and I knew it.

The counselor came straight out and told me what she thought that was about. She said, "You're obsessed with this because of what happened to you when you were a kid means everything to you. Your whole ideal of sex is important and significant in your relationship. That's why you're so obsessed with that whole aspect."

I still had that horrible feeling that I couldn't erase my obsession without facing the details for myself. If I could do it all over again, not that I would want to, I would have gone straight to her boyfriend and gotten the answers and closed the case. People say not to ask questions you don't want the answers to. But that was the process I had to go through to get over it. Now that I'm older, if I have a suspicion I'll investigate. I'll find proof. Because I can't get less than the truth.

Catelynn:

Since counseling, I can't handle lying! There are still times when I struggle with the reflex to be dishonest. There are a lot of times when lies come out automatically, without me even thinking about it. My mouth opens and I just blurt out whatever lie pops off of the tip of my tongue. It's such a deep habit that I haven't gotten enough distance from it yet. But now, after I say something dishonest, my heart will start racing until I have so much anxiety that I have to come clean.

One therapist told us that was a normal part of the learning process. When I explained to her that I couldn't stomach lying anymore but was still struggling with this automatic reaction to blurt out the kind of crap I was used to saying, the therapist told Tyler that was a normal part of it. She said, "Sometimes Cate might need five minutes to think about it and work through her reaction." For me, because the roots of my lying are based in feeling unsafe, sometimes I need extra time to find a way to say something that makes me feel safe. And still, sometimes my mouth just vomits words and then five minutes later I think, "Shit, I just lied about that." Then I'll turn to Tyler and say, "I'm sorry, babe. That wasn't true. This is the truth." And that requires me to have trust in him not to get so mad that he'll yell at me and leave.

Tyler:

The counselor told me, "Your job is to make her feel safe enough to tell you the truth. So whatever you have to do to make her feel comfortable and safe and confident to tell you the truth, that's what you need to do." And that went along with me having to work on my reaction. I'm almost too honest and blunt sometimes, and I'll say whatever I'm thinking or feeling when it's not really necessary. So I had to work on my reactions to what she said. If I freak out when I'm unhappy, she's not going to feel safe telling me the truth. And really, that's not hard for me to relate to. I've always demanded that people hear my side of the story before they judge me. So I can learn to do the same thing from my end.

Catelynn:

A lot of relationships end because of trust. Once it's broken once, you can't get it back. You have to make a habit of honesty in your relationship and you have to make each other feel safe. It had to be a team effort. If he has a problem, what am I doing to fuel that problem? If I have a problem, what's he doing to fuel my problem? How can we help each other instead of escalating this?

Tyler:

Lying is a deal breaker for a lot of people, and it was for me, too. But I learned that's not really the best approach. I really want people to know that lying is fixable. Just because someone lies doesn't mean that you're not meant to be with that person, or that the lying will go on forever. It's a fixable issue.

You can't just say, "Oh, he lied, that's it, he's not the person for me." I remember mentioning to the couples' therapist that I thought I should have just left and been done with it. But whoever thinks love is like a sappy movie with no challenges is dead wrong. Love is work. And when people say "If you have to work on it it's not love," I'm like, what world are you living in?

As far as trust and communication go, those are all things that take work. You don't naturally just communicate, you're not naturally honest. Those things take work. Your relationship is a really valuable thing that has a lot of different parts to it. Why would you throw away the whole thing based on one broken part? You have to at least try to repair it. What if I had left Catelynn for something that could have been fixed? I would never have the relationship and happiness I have now.

Closing Thoughts

From the very beginning, we have had a very special chemistry and passion for each other. Even when we were twelve, we knew. You know when you're soulmates. You know when you can picture being with that person for the rest of your life. Placing Carly left us with more time to find the peace, maturity and wisdom together to start a family and do it right. It gave us room to work for the goal of making it until we're eighty-seven, hanging out in rocking chairs.

That being said, every relationship is going to have its ups and downs, even when two people have never doubted for a second that they are soulmates. Because when you get down to it, relationships are hard. Whether it's the relationship between you and your parents, your friends, or a significant other.

Relationships take communication, understanding, and compromise. Those are three things we thought we had nailed down, and maybe we did. But life catches up with you. Cate's lying almost got the best of us. There's no doubt about it that our relationship was put to the ultimate test. It was make it or break it time and we knew we couldn't live with ourselves if we just let it all fall to pieces.

Without couple's counseling we probably wouldn't have learned that Tyler's obsession with sex was linked to his childhood sexual abuse. Cate's lying started to make sense given the dysfunctional household she grew up in. It was much easier for her to lie to avoid conflict than to risk the repercussions of being honest. Before sifting through these issues Cate's lying just seemed like something she did to be deceptive or hurtful. Tyler was able to start making sense of his obsession with sex. By working through these issues as a totally united team we were able to be there for each other in ways we never had been before.

Nobody is perfect, so there will always be hurdles. Sometimes they're big and sometimes they're small. Working through our problems in therapy was a turning point for us. By going to therapy we picked up the tools we needed to put the past behind us and move forward.

Even if you think there's a problem in your relationship that can't be fixed, it never hurts to try. It might be painful, and it will definitely be difficult, but if your relationship is worth fighting for, you'll be glad you did!

CHAPTER 9:

PLANNING A HAPPY HOME

All of our dreams and efforts after Carly boiled down to our ideas about what makes a good home for a child. What does a child need to grow up to be a good person? When we wrote down all the things in our lives that wouldn't be good for a child, the sum total was enough to make our decision. But there wasn't any single thing on that list that was a deal breaker. We never believed it was impossible to raise a child in poverty, for example. We never thought that a person who'd struggled with addiction couldn't step up to be a parent. We didn't want to raise our kid in a trailer park, but that doesn't mean we had less respect for the moms, like ours, who had done that same thing.

Although we've had to take an honest look at how our family dysfunction affected our lives, we never once questioned the love and good intentions of the people who raised us. No one gets to design a perfect life. There are many amazing, wonderful parents out there who are doing the best they can for their children while struggling with poverty, family addiction, and other circumstances beyond their control.

We talk a lot about escaping the legacies of our backgrounds, and how our family troubles showed us what not to do. But we also have to acknowledge the positive. After all, can we really take all the credit for breaking the cycle? So many teenagers – including some of our parents and grandparents before us – have walked the same line we walked and fallen onto the wrong side. What made us different? Was it just luck that gave us the strength to make the decisions we made? Were we just born with a different attitude? We don't know the answers to those questions. But we do know that at least in part, we are products of our environment. Just like our parents were products of their environments, and their parents were before that. Carly's environment will have a hand in shaping who she becomes, and when we have our next child, the environment we provide for her will impact the person she becomes.

With every generation, families teach children lessons good and bad. What lessons have we learned? What did we inherit from our parents that we want to pass down? Are we safe now from the flaws and faults that have held back so many generations of our family? What new insights can we bring to our turn of the cycle? How will we build and protect our dream of a happy home?

Money Isn't Everything

Catelynn:

Let's make one thing absolutely clear. Poverty was a factor in our decision to place Carly in adoption, but being poor does *not* make you a bad parent. Money problems can happen to anyone, and when you're born into them, they're even harder to escape. My mom never had anyone to turn to for backup when money was tight. But she worked her ass off to take care of us. And whatever luxury we didn't have, she made up for in love. We have all the respect and love in the world for the parents out there who are living paycheck to paycheck, pouring all their energy into providing for their kids.

Tyler:

Being a single mom is the hardest job in the world. End of story. (The second hardest job, by the way, is just being a mom at all!) Cate and I are both children of single moms who basically came from nothing, got pregnant unexpectedly, and struggled for the rest of their lives to make ends meet while providing for their children.

When I was really little, my mom and sister and I were living in a dilapidated trailer park in the back of a dead end street. That place was full of poverty-stricken families, and our family was one of them. It was so destitute that our playground was a rusted-out broken tractor at the east end of the trailer park.

My mom worked herself to the bone to get us out of there. She worked day and night, saving up all the tips from her bartending job at a local golf course, until she had enough money to move us into this tiny seven-hundred square foot cottage that just barely passed as a house. My mom worked her ass off for that place.

Catelynn:

For my mom, the big thing was being financially independent. That was an advantage she fought for. For a lot of young moms who grew up in bad environments, it's easy to fall into the trap of having to rely on a man for money. And that can lead to all kinds of bad situations. Just look what happened with Detroit. When she didn't have her own place to go back to, she got sucked into a nightmare it took her a year to escape. For a lot of women like her, that nightmare never ends. But for my mom it was a wrong turn that she knew she had to make right. Before and after that, my mom always worked hard to have her own house and pay her own bills. And even though she had a habit of letting guys mooch off her, I remember her kicking out at least one boyfriend who wouldn't pay his half of the bills. She really did the best she could to stay in control of what little money she had. Sure, her house was a trailer, but it was hers and hers alone. And no matter how bad her addiction was, it never kept her home from work. I can remember waking up two hours before school so she could drop us off with a babysitter and get to her job. She worked her butt off every day to take care of us the best way she knew how, and that's something I'll always admire.

Tyler:

My mom was really open about our finances. If I said I wanted something and we couldn't afford it, she'd say no. And when I asked why, she'd tell me. "That's ten dollars, and I only have five dollars right now." Some parents don't like to talk about money with their kids, so in that situation, they would say, "You can't have it, because I said so." But my mom's honesty helped me understand: I want this, but I can't have it because my mom doesn't have money. I agree that you should never burden your kids with financial stress, and my mom never walked around the house crying and ranting about being able to pay the bills. But if I asked for something we couldn't have, she told me the truth.

But we always had Christmas, and we also got treats and splurges. Sometimes even when money was tight, my mom would turn to my sister and me and say, "We're going to Olive Garden tonight. We're going to have a nice dinner and spend time as a family." We'd ask, how are you going to afford that? And she'd say, "I don't care if I'm broke for the rest of the week. We're not going to worry about money tonight." She was careful with finances, but never at the cost of spending quality time with us or making a happy memory. In her eyes, money was nothing compared to that.

The Power of Love

Catelynn:

I had a rough childhood. We've already established that. But no matter which busted-up trailer park we were living in, there was always love in our house. My mom was always loving. She always gave us hugs, telling us we were beautiful, and making sure we knew how much she cared about us. No matter what's happened, I've never doubted that my mom loved me.

That was something she never had. My mom grew up being treated like an unwanted piece of trash. No one hugged her or built up her self-esteem. When I hear about it, it sounds to me like she took a lot of damage for the ugly divorce her parents went through. All the anger and frustration got taken out on her. She's told me stories of trying to go up and give one of her parents a hug, and just being pushed away. She'd get punished for the dumbest things, just basically being bullied as a scapegoat for an unhappy house. That left a really deep mark on her. I think that's the reason for a lot of the problems she's struggled with in her adult life. How is a young girl supposed to cope with feeling unloved and unwanted? Drinking probably helped her detach from those problems so she could have fun and act like a normal, outgoing person. I don't blame her for that.

I don't know what I would have been like if I'd gone all my life feeling unloved. And the reason I never found out was because my mom knew how it affected her, and she made sure she made up for it with her own kids. We got hugs. We got kindness. We got those expressions of love. And in a way, even though she wasn't able to break the cycle herself, sometimes I wonder if those changes she made paved the way for me to do it. I know they definitely meant something.

Tyler:

Growing up, there was never a single day when my mom didn't tell me she loved me. Even when we got in fights, she'd find a way to work it in there that she was only upset because she loved me and she wanted the best for me. There were times when we'd argue on the phone and hang up really mad, and then I'd realized we'd forgotten to say it. I'd almost be in tears until I called her back to say I loved her. There was an unspoken rule that we could never leave anything negative hanging without making that expression. You never know what could happen. So no matter what the situation was, the final note was always love.

Good and Bad Examples

Tyler:

One of the many things Cate and I have in common is we both have parents who are total opposites. So we got really mixed influences growing up.

Catelynn:

I think I was about nine months old when my mom and dad split up, and my mom's party lifestyle had a lot to do it. Don't get me wrong, there's nothing wrong with a little partying! It's cool if you never party, but lots of people have their wild and crazy phase when they're young. We did, and we don't regret it. But when I was born my dad thought differently about what he was doing. Obviously my mom did too but they were both still young parents, it was all a learning process.

My dad stayed close to me, though. We spent a lot of time together until I was twelve, when he had to move out of state. My dad's cool. He's the most normal person in the world. I have no memories of my dad being under the influence of anything. There was never any chaos where he was concerned. He's just a naturally chill, laid-back person, like me.

I was definitely a daddy's girl when I was a kid. He was the type of guy who never missed a visit with me. Every Wednesday we'd get lunch after school, and every other weekend I'd go over to his house. We'd go on drives and go tromping around in the woods together, just spending time together and talking. Back in those days, I wasn't acting up yet. But later, even though he was all the way down in Florida, he always tried to talk to me about doing well in school and how important my education was.

I always looked at him and his parents as the biggest positive influence in my life. They weren't there in Michigan with me, but the older I got the more I felt them pushing me to do good things in my life. It was so important for me to have that, especially because they were the ones who stepped in when my home life was at its most chaotic. They took me in when my own home wasn't safe for awhile, and they supported me all through my pregnancy. Their love and understanding made it easy to be open to their guidance, and I really leaned on that positive influence in those years Tyler and I were fighting to turn our lives around.

Tyler:

My mom generally always had her shit together. She listened to her parents and got good grades. She might have partied here and there, but just like a normal teenage girl. She was a good kid who liked to have a good time. She caught my dad's eye while he was riding by on his bike one day. And of course he's always been a smooth talker. That night he charmed her into climbing onto the back of his bike with him, and eventually she fell in love. Once they got together, she started going out more to keep up with him. Even back then, he was into more serious stuff than weed, but my mom never really got too involved with it. At least not enough to take her life off course.

Their love lost to his hard-partying ways, though. After my sister was born, my mom spent a lot of time waiting around, staying up all night, wondering where he was or if he was okay. Eventually she realized there was an addiction in the house, and she didn't want that in our lives. So they were already separated before I was born. But one night my dad went through a crisis and my mom got a little too close as she offered support. I was conceived during a temporary reunion. They were never together during my life, and not long after I was born, he was in prison.

The Value of Trust

Catelynn:

My favorite thing about my mom was that I could talk to her about anything. Our relationship only got rocky after Carly. Before that, we were very close. I could always tell her what was going on in my life, and she never judged me. When I lost my virginity and didn't tell her right away, she was almost in tears because I hadn't felt like I could confide in her. As a young girl, I had just been scared to admit that I'd made that choice. But she told me, "You could have come to me and talked to me and told me about it!" She was very open with me, and she wanted me to be open with her. Parents should give kids that sense that they're going to listen and give advice and not judge them.

Tyler:

It always meant a lot to me that my mom listened to my side of every story. Like I explained way back in the beginning of the book, it was important to her that I trusted her enough to tell me what was happening in my life when she wasn't there. That was why when I told her a teacher wasn't giving the whole story, she never shut me down. She listened and investigated for herself. Thanks to that, I was never scared she'd take someone else's word over mine and she could rest easy knowing no one would do something bad to her son without her hearing about it.

Catelynn and I both agree that our children have to know, one hundred percent, that our home is their safe zone. You leave the world at the front door. Home is where you can be yourself without any judgment. Catelynn and I know that our children will always have that safety.

Raising "Good Kids"

Catelynn:

My mom and I got along so well we were like best friends. We never fought, and I never disrespected her or raised my voice to her. But our relationship might not have been the best as far as rules and boundaries went. She let me do whatever I wanted! I had no restrictions at all as a kid, and very little supervision. I'm lucky I turned out the way I did! The way I was running around and the stuff I was getting away with, I could have been pregnant at the age of 12. If I had made a few different choices and gone along with some of the stuff my friends and neighbors did, I could have turned out just like everybody around me.

My time with my grandparents in Florida balanced that out. They were so strict I didn't even know how to take it! Of course, I can understand their motives for it. They were just taking care of me and trying to keep me out of trouble, and that was some good instincts on their part considering all the stuff I'd already done! They didn't know about all of my wild stuff, though. At least, I don't think they did. But they knew what kind of environment I was coming from, and they had front-row seats to how chaotic my life was getting. They were right to try and lay some boundaries down. I've always had respect for the ways they pushed me to be good.

Tyler:

My mom tried to teach me to act right, but obviously I had a hard time falling in line all through school. She even had me see a counselor to try and see if there was a reason for all the behavior trouble. I was in counseling from eight or nine up until the age of fifteen, but the only disorder they could really come up with was just plain old acting up. Part of it, I think, was the effects of not having my dad around. I was raised in a household full of women, and I was cool with that, but at the same time I had to figure out on my own what it meant to act like a man. I wanted to establish myself, be strong and assert my opinions, and I was always looking for ways to be tough. But honestly, when it gets right down to it. I think I was just born with a strong will and an idea of what was right, and I was never able to go along with things that didn't make sense to me.

But what happens if our child follows our "bad kid" footsteps? Cate and I talk about what we'll do if we have a kid like me, a kid who just can't keep his mouth shut. And you know what? It might sound crazy, but a part of me doesn't want my kid to be a perfect goody-good kid. A part of me is like, "God, please, don't give me a boring kid!" I pray no child of mine will ever be out doing crazy stuff and hurting themselves, but I also don't want a kid who says "Yes daddy, yes teacher" without thinking for themselves about whether what's happening is right and wrong.

We want to leave room for our kid to be strong, to have a sense of what's fair and when to speak up. And if that means going out there and getting in trouble once in awhile, so be it, as long as they're learning from those experiences. If that means a few detentions or suspensions, we'll live with it. The fact is, any kid with strong opinions probably isn't going to make it through twelve years of school without some kind of clash with authority!

The problem kids might act up and do things they're not supposed to do, but so many times, there's something more beneath the surface. They have a spark. They have a kind of energy other kids don't have. When they're younger, they don't know how to show that spark without pissing people off — especially if they haven't had somebody take the extra time to teach them. But when they get older, if they can learn to channel whatever it is that makes it hard for them to fall in line, that spark can be the thing that makes him special.

I don't want to smother that spark. I want to give them the freedom and the guidance to build their character. And if they make some messes or take some wrong turns, I'll do what my mom did. I'll ask what happened, I'll ask what they were feeling when they caused that trouble. I'll try and make that spark into something positive.

Living Up to a Promise

Tyler:

When we talk about Nova, we talk about how we want her to constantly know how loved she is. We want to tell her every day, and not just tell her but show her in the way we live our lives and run our household. Weirdly, Cate and I are just waiting for the thing we don't agree on. But our morals and values have sort of blended in the years we've been together. Being old friends makes a huge difference in that way, because we spent the hardest times of our lives together, developing together. We've been through the wringer. But we've always gotten through it as a team, and we're determined to keep that going when we're parenting our child.

We've already decided one parent cannot undermine the other parent. If mom and dad don't agree, they need to put their heads together. And then we can have a family meeting. And if they can't come to an agreement, then you change into jeans. Nova will never just come up to me and ask for permission. I will ask mom. It's going to be cooperative. We have to stay a team.

Catelynn:

I have always wanted a happy, stable home. That's what I've wanted all my life, and I'm never going to compromise that dream. It's a promise to myself, a promise to Tyler, and a promise to our children. Tyler and I confirm it with each other all the time. We look at each other and say, "We're going to make this work, and we're going to raise this little girl together, and this is how it's going to be. We're going to have bumps in the road, but we're going to make it. Period."

Our bond in that is really our belief that once we take responsibility for a child, every decision has to be made with our child's best interest in mind. We want Nova and all of our children after her to know that anything we do in our lives is about her. Everything is going to be about this kid. We'll never put our own selfish impulses in front of her essential needs for love and stability. The times of living our lives only for ourselves will be done the moment she's born. Everything has to be about the baby. Whatever happens after she's born, everything is for her.

Tyler:

A good parent is willing to sacrifice for their child, regardless of what momentary pleasure or convenience it costs them. Someone who doesn't act and do things selfishly, but parents selflessly, *that* is a parent. And we know that's a hard commitment to make. But it's always harder to do the right thing than the wrong thing. If the right thing was always easy, everyone would do it!

Closing Thoughts

Growing up, no matter how bad certain circumstances may have been, we always knew we were loved. Even during the most difficult times we were lucky enough to have moms that always worked their asses off and consistently showed us how much they loved us. That's why we both have all the respect in the world for the women who raised us. They taught us how to be kind, loving people. We don't doubt that we will be great parents because of everything we learned from them.

Our moms were always there for us. We could go to them and be completely honest and open about anything we were going through because we trusted them and they respected us. That's the kind of relationship we want to have with our children. Of course, it wasn't always rainbows and butterflies. We also learned from dysfunction the kind of parents we don't want to be.

We both know how hard it can be to grow up with just one parent in the picture and we never want our daughter to have to experience that. We want to be a team, two parents who are always there for our children. Will we make mistakes? Hell yes! Every parent does. But we're doing our best to learn from the generations before us. We're fighting not to make the same mistakes blindly, and we've prepared ourselves to own up to whatever screw-ups we do stumble into.

We decided to place Carly in adoption when we realized we couldn't provide the home that she deserved. In the years since making that choice, we've had even more time to look back on our family histories and think about how we will do things differently. We reflected on things like Cate's mom's struggle with addiction and how Tyler's dad's absence from his life deeply affected him. The last thing we wanted was to perpetuate that cycle of dysfunction, poverty, and addiction. All of the pain and heartbreak we experienced growing up shaped the way we will raise our daughter.

We know that providing a good home is not about money or being able to spoil your kid. A good home is a safe zone with healthy boundaries and rules based on understanding. When it comes to raising our children, we want to be a united front, a team. We want her to know that we will always be there for her and that she can come to us for advice, support, and encouragement. Most of all, we want her to be surrounded by love so that she always feels safe and secure. Our daughter won't go one day without hearing the three most important words a parent can say to a child: "I love you." And if she ever wants proof of those words, we'll do our best to make sure all she has to do is look around at the home we've made.

CHAPTER 10:

TAKING RESPONSIBILITY

When we tell our story, we talk a lot about sacrifice. We talk about breaking the cycle. We talk about overcoming chaos and conquering bad habits and influences. But maybe the best way to sum up our efforts over these past years is that we've tried to take responsibility for our lives. We've tried to remember that we are in control of our lives, our choices, our mistakes, and our behavior. We decide what kind of people we want to be. And even though we can look at our environments and find ways to explain why we weren't exactly angels when we were younger, in the end we have to own our mistakes and take responsibility for what we do.

As we write this book, we're expecting our second daughter, Nova. It's never been more important for us to think about who we are and how to live healthy, positive lives. Because we know that parents have the most responsibility of all. We want to raise our daughter with the values we've fought to build. We want to teach her by example how to be an honest person who tries her best to do the right thing, even when it's not the easiest thing. We want her to know that the best life you can possibly have is one you take full responsibility for. Every person chooses who they'll be and what kind of life they'll live. That's an awesome thing.

We want to share some of our own experiences and ideas about taking responsibility. There are so many different ways it's played out in our lives. But learning to take responsibility has been one of the most important factors in conquering chaos in our lives. And when anyone asks us for advice, that's usually the mindset we're coming from.

Be Your Own Champion First

Tyler:

Your self-esteem is your responsibility. It's no one else's job to make you love yourself. People rely on others a lot to make them feel good, especially in their relationships. But if you feel bad about yourself, you shouldn't count on a relationship to change that. Of course your partner should be someone who boosts your self-esteem and make you feel better about yourself. But it's not their responsibility to create your self-worth from scratch. It's not their responsibility to give your life all of its meaning. No one can do that for you.

Catelynn and I talked about that a lot whenever we discussed getting married. Of course everyone has their own issues with confidence and self-esteem. Not everyone completely loves themselves. But Catelynn and I strongly agree: "It's not your job to make me happy. It's not my job to make you happy. Our jobs are to love each other, support each other, and uplift each other. But we're still responsible for our own happiness."

Catelynn:

You have to have your own self-love before you can accept love in a healthy way. You can't have all of your self-worth wrapped up in another person. That's dangerous! You shouldn't have to rely on others for that. You should be happy yourself, and the other person should be an added bonus.

It's hard to get over your insecurities alone. There are people out there hurting and feeling bad about themselves. They're looking for a partner to save them. But that's the unhealthiest way to do that. You need to feel self-worth before you get into a relationship. When you put your self-esteem in someone else's hands, what happens if they mess up and drop it?

First of all, you have to grasp that it's your problem. Someone else might have started it in you, but now you're the only one who can fix it. It's no one else's responsibility. It's hard to face your demons and come to grips with stuff. But it needs to be done. Get counseling. Get down deep into why you have self-esteem problems. Learn self-worth exercises to help you feel better about yourself. It's so frustrating if all someone does is complain about their insecurities and then doesn't try to fix them. If you have insecurities, work on them! They don't have to bring your life down.

The insecurity I struggled with was my weight. I've always thought I was too big or too curvy. I think I know where it came from. Starting when I was four years old, there was a woman in my dad's family who would pick at my weight when I visited. Every time I saw her she would say something like, "Oh, you're getting chunky!" She would even lecture me about dieting, telling me, "You shouldn't eat that, too many calories!" My mom remembers once I got home from a visit from my dad, my mom had some donuts as a treat to welcome me back. Apparently I said, "Oh, sorry, mom. There are too many calories in donuts. I can't have any of those." My mom was furious!

My mom always told me I was beautiful when I was growing up. I got a lot of positive messages. But I was still always insecure about my weight. I've never worn short shorts or bikinis in my entire life. Even when I've lost weight and been pretty thin, I've always felt fat. That image of myself never goes away. That's something most girls with insecurities about their appearances will understand. Even if you're down to the weight you wanted to be at, even at a size two, your insecurity still tells you you're not skinny. It's never driven me insane or made me depressed, but it's always been there in my mind.

Tyler:

I remember the first time I heard about that insecurity of Cate's. We were having a kind of difficult talk about my ex-girlfriend, and Catelynn was crying, and offhand she said, "I'm not skinny-minny like your other girlfriend!" That caught me off guard. Of course she wasn't as skinny as that girl, but I always thought she looked better! So it really jumped out at me when she showed me that she was insecure with that. But I never forgot it. Once I knew it was something she struggled with, I always made sure to be sensitive about it and tell her she was beautiful.

I have the opposite insecurity. I hate being skinny! It's funny, because since our insecurities are totally different, neither of us would have guessed what the other one struggled with. I can't imagine wanting to be skinnier. And Cate can't imagine feeling too skinny. She sometimes jokes to me, "I wish I had your problem!" And I'm like, "No! Curves are my thing!" But actually, that's why it was important that we were open with each other about those insecurities. If we weren't, we might accidentally hurt each other's feelings. For example, if Catelynn didn't know I was insecure about being skinny, she might say something like, "Wow, Tyler, you look skinny today!" She would have no idea that would be really negative to me. I might say, "Whoa, you look so curvy in those jeans!" I wouldn't know she would be hurt by that.

So you have to lay those insecurities bare in your relationship. It's really scary to put yourself in a vulnerable place, but that's how you start to work through things together. We confront those self-esteem problems, and we know how to uplift each other. We don't try to fix each other, but we make sure to stay positive wherever the other person has trouble doing it. When Catelynn spends time getting ready and dressing up, it's my job to say, "Wow, you look beautiful." And when I joke around and call myself a skinny bastard, it's Cate's job to say, "Don't say that! You're hot!" It works out.

Catelynn:

We're good at motivating each other to do good and praising each other. Since we try to be honest about the difficult things, it's even more important to be open with positive input. That way we're not afraid to hurt each other's feelings when we have to talk about something nega-tive, because we've built up an understanding that we're thinking the best toward each other. I wouldn't try to hurt him and he wouldn't try to hurt me. So we can be open, with that foundation of trust.

One good thing about being with someone in a relationship is that they uplift you. That's one thing they should always do. No one's going to come on a white horse and fix your problem, but you can always count on them to support you in that job. Never the opposite. If someone you're with bashes you and brings your self-esteem down, that's unhealthy. If you're in a relationship like that, you need to get out. Your partner should be lifting you up and boosting your self-esteem. That's your job in any relationship, too. If you notice someone damaging your self-worth and self-esteem, leave.

Tyler:

There should never be low blows in a relationship. I'm always shocked when I hear friends fighting and they throw so many low blows. That's not allowed between us. If I trust you enough to show you where I'm vulnerable, you are not allowed to use it against me. If I tell you I hate being skinny and a week later you call me a scrawny bastard when you're mad, then I know your intention was to hurt me. And that's not how a good relationship works at all. Some people use their emotional state as an excuse for making mean remarks to their partner, like they couldn't help going there because they were so upset. But that's no excuse for saying something that actually hurts your partner. Think what you have to, in that case, but keep it in your head where it doesn't hurt anybody. My grandma used to tell me, "Only God can hear your thoughts, but the Devil hears your voice."

You should never be afraid to expose your vulnerabilities to your partner, or think they'll use your honesty against you later. So actually, being open with your vulnerabilities does two things: It gives the other person a way to uplift you, and it gives you a chance to spot a red flag if they use it against you. Give someone your kryptonite. Then if they use it again, you know to get out of there. And if you've built up your own armor against it, your own self-worth, you'll be okay.

Of course, we're being grown-ups here. When it comes to children, they absolutely need all the help they can get building their early self-esteem. We're going to uplift our children constantly. I want to tell them how beautiful they are. When I think about Cate's insecurity and how common that is with girls, it makes me want to work extra hard to make sure Nova's self-esteem is as strong as it can be. Fathers have a huge role in the way daughters feel about themselves. For a girl, your dad is the first relationship you have with the opposite sex. So how he treats you has a huge part to do with how you'll expect to be treated by men in the future and your ideas about how they see you. It's a dad's responsibility to tell his daughter she's beautiful, strong, and important.

Catelynn:

Kids should never get negative messages about their appearance. I hate to hear kids getting criticized by adults for such vulnerable things. When you're a kid, those careless remarks can cause permanent damage. When that woman from my childhood singled me out for my weight, I never forgot about it. I always felt like an outcast in that part of the family, like I didn't look good enough for their standards. That should never happen! It's the adults' responsibility to make sure kids are developing a positive image of themselves. No one should ever be singled out for criticism on something so sensitive.

Treating Others With Respect

Catelynn:

There's one thing we both have to take responsibility for that's hard to own up to. We talk positive now, but back when we were in grade school, we both went through a phase when we could be really mean to other kids. We were bullies, to put it bluntly. It's so uncomfortable to think about it, because we know the effects bullying can have on people for the rest of their lives. And we both grew out of the phase when we were still young, so it's even harder to make sense of. I can't remember a time when I ever felt like it was fun to be mean to someone. But obviously there was a time like that.

There was this boy from the trailer park who I used to beat up every day at the bus stop. I was so mean to that kid, and for no reason! We had this creek that ran by the place, and I'm not sure I'd even want to call it a creek. It was nasty and smelly, with green slime all along the sides. We used to play around it sometimes, putting boards across like a bridge and walking back and forth. And one day, for no reason at all, I just pushed this boy into that nasty, stinky creek. I feel horrible remembering that.

Tyler:

I started bullying kids in kindergarten. I remember picking on the kid who sat next to me in class. Every day I'd pick a moment where this kid wasn't paying attention. Then I'd take my little scissors, cut a hole in his shirt and laugh my ass off. The kid would beg me to stop: "My mom's getting mad, all of my shirts have holes!" God, I was a little dick. There was another kid named Rob who I was even worse to. I'd pretend to be his friend, take him to a park, and then push him around and beat him up. I'd apologize the next day and pretend to be friends, and then I'd do it again.

I was such an asshole. I was so mean! I've spent a lot of time thinking about it. I feel really bad about what I did. A few years ago I managed to find Rob on Facebook and sent him a long apology. I said, "I know I'm probably the last person you want to hear from, but I was the kid who used to beat you up." I expressed how wrong I was and how bad I felt for doing that. I told him I had to find him because I couldn't live with myself for the rest of my life without apologizing. He never wrote me back.

I was mean until about fourth grade. And then I went the opposite way and started feeling really, really bad for people. Then I started turning my aggression toward the bullies instead of being one myself. Once we got a new girl at school who was African-American, she was the only black kid there. Imagine what that's like, to be the only black girl in the middle of a bunch of trailer park kids in one of the whitest parts of Michigan. Sure enough, this one boy started in on her, calling her the N-word. After I saw that going on, I took that kid into the bathroom and told him I'd kick his ass if he ever picked on her again. After that I started being nice to everyone and going out of my way to be nice to people who weren't being treated right. You never know how much good you can do for someone just by giving them some positive attention that day.

Catelynn:

When I got older, I changed, too. We just went through these phases. I don't know where it stemmed from, whether it was related to some of the stuff we were going through in our family lives, or what. Maybe it was a way to take out the aggression we were holding in for ourselves. There's no excuse, though, and the explanation doesn't matter to the kids we were mean to. They were the ones who were hurt by it. When I grew up a little, I turned my attitude in the other direction, too. I'd stand up for people who were getting picked on, and I didn't let my friends do that to people, either. Once I was just old enough to think about it, I had no desire to be cruel to anyone. How is that fun to hurt people? I'm heartbroken that I ever did. I can't take it back, but take full responsibility for it. All I can do is make sure I never act like that again in my life, and teach my children that bullying is never okay.

These days we find ourselves on the receiving end of mean behavior and careless comments. After we appeared on TV, after the first huge rush of positive responses, we definitely had to deal with a lot of negativity. We had no idea what kind of attention was going to come our way when we decided to do that show. The internet could be a horrible place. People were always saying I was fat, calling me ugly, tweeting at Tyler to leave me and be with them. Prank callers would find my number, call me and tell me they were pregnant with Tyler's baby. Random girls were always trying to start psycho stuff.

It got to the point where I didn't want to go out to clubs or anything. Bitches were crazy! I was afraid something would go down and my old trailer park side would come out. I didn't want to be tempted to end up beating somebody's ass for going after my man. There definitely were people who tried to start trouble when we were out. Once after we'd gone out dancing, Tyler told me some girl was feeling up his thigh when he was there with me on the dance floor. I was like, "You should have just told me!" But he said, "What? I wasn't going to tell you! You would have whooped her ass!" He did the right thing and kicked her off, though.

The girls pull that crap online, too, sending Tyler messages and trying to be sexy. I don't understand ladies these days. Have respect for other women. These girls see us together. They know we're a couple. They just don't have respect. What would they do if I treated them like that? And the things they write in public about our relationship are so vicious. Now that we've been at this TV thing for several years, we know better than to read things. But in the beginning it was hard to ignore it.

Tyler:

I don't know what the motivation is behind some of the messages I get, because it's not attractive. Some of these girls seem to assume all guys are the same. Like, they shake their asses and the guys will crumble. And there have been a few times I got so fed up with some stupid message I wrote back and kind of went off. I'd be like, "I don't know what you think you're getting out of this, but it's not working for me at all. All this tells me is that you have no self-respect." Why would they present themselves like that? The woman I love has strong values. She made me work for it. I'm not interested in someone who's going to try and pick me up when I'm obviously in a relationship. And when these girls tell me I can do better than her, I get pissed. You have no idea who she is. And who are you to tell me who I can be with? Why do you care, anyway? It amazes me that people are so invested in this. Why do they give a shit who I'm with? I'm not gonna be with the girl who grabs my leg in the club while I'm dancing with my girl.

The internet makes people feel like they can be as rude as they want without any consequence. They take no responsibility for the effect their stupid comment might have on the person it's about. When the show first came out, Twitter wasn't what it is now. Now everyone's on there giving instant feedback. They look at us as a conversation topic or an easy target to attack. Instagram is like the devil's playground for cyber-bullying. I can post a picture of my dog, and it'll turn into "You're ugly." The thing about it is, people comment on all this stuff, but would you say that to someone you know? We're people. We're human beings. We're in the public eye, but we're actual people with actual feelings. They're not getting the emotional consequences or a physical response. They just comment. They think it does nothing to someone. But I guarantee they would never do that to my face.

Owning Your Behavior

Catelynn:

A lot of people use their environments and backgrounds as excuses for what's wrong with their lives. We know as well as anybody that family problems, broken homes, and bad role models can push your life in the wrong direction. But from the moment you're able to look around and see what's good and bad in your life, it's your responsibility to take care of whatever is in your control. When Cate and I made that crazy transition from trailer park delinquents to responsible teenagers, we did it in the same environment that had fostered our worst behavior. People always say that in order to change, you have to cut all negative influences out of your life. It's true that if you can do that, you should. But don't use that advice to make excuses for not changing, like you can't make better decisions if someone's not leading you by the hand. And if there's someone around who always "gets you into trouble," it's on you to learn how to be around that person and not fall into that trap. Don't blame them. They don't control your brain or the choices you make. Your friends and family may play a part in what you do, but once you know right from wrong, you need to take responsibility for doing what's right.

Tyler:

Sometimes that means you have to pass on things that other people choose for themselves. One thing that was hard for us to deal with after

Carly was when our friends started having babies. They came from the same messed-up backgrounds we came from, but they decided to make a go of it and keep their babies. When we saw that, it brought out a lot of painful feelings from the part of us that almost didn't make the decision we made. You make this decision, you plan for it, you make peace with it, and then you're faced with someone who chose the thing you didn't. It's not like you regret what you did, but you have a petty sort of moment of, "Well they're doing it. Why couldn't I do it?" It was hard to see people having kids as young as we were and parenting. Of course we had our fantasies and daydreams about what it would be like to have her with us. Watching our friends make the choice we didn't make brought up all of our "What ifs." But we made our own decision based on our own situation and our own understanding of what the right thing to do was. Taking responsibility for that decisions means pushing through those painful moments of, "That person has this thing I want. Why can't I have that?"

Closing Thoughts

Taking responsibility for your life isn't always easy. Whether it's owning up to your mistakes or holding up your end of a relationship, recognizing that you're in charge of your life comes with pressure and tough decisions. But it also puts you in the position to make the most of yourself and your life.

It's the same as understanding what it means to know right from wrong. We talk about this all the time. When there's a right thing to do and a wrong thing to do, the right thing usually isn't the easier option. That's why people screw up. It's easy to screw up! It's easy to act on impulse, to be selfish, to do the thing that feels the best right at this moment. But when you make the effort to do the right thing instead, you see the consequences are so much better in the end. When you're honest and kind to people, they trust you more. When you're fair and own up to your mistakes, you get more respect. And when you put someone else's needs before your own, you get to be a part of their happiness as a result.

Taking responsibility for your life is the same thing. No matter how hard it is to own your behavior, that's the only way you'll ever get the most out of life. If you don't like yourself, make yourself into the kind of person you respect. If you don't like your life, find out what you can change to make it more like the life you want. If you've wronged someone, apologize and give yourself and them a way to move on. And if you ever get the urge to just act up and be selfish, remember it's not worth compromising the person you want to be!

CHAPTER 11:

A CHANCE
TO INSPIRE

We are on an incredible journey. There have been times when we felt overwhelmed, helpless, and uncertain. There have been disappointments, difficult challenges, and painful sacrifices. But when we made the decision to choose right over wrong and fight for a better life, we opened ourselves to more positivity, happiness, and hope than we ever imagined.

Our efforts have already paid off in the form of so many wonderful blessings. Our first child is in a safe, happy home, surrounded by great role models, and we know she's getting the chance to pursue every opportunity she deserves. In the years since we placed Carly in adoption, we've had our own opportunity to grow into the kind of people we want to be for our children. And the most unexpected gift of all is that we've had the chance to share our story with the world and connect with people who can benefit from it.

Since our experience with teen pregnancy and adoption first aired on MTV, we've heard from so many people who were touched by our journey. With the help of Dawn, the adoption counselor who guided us through the adoption process and has continued to support us and Carly's adoptive parents, we began to share our story with people in person through speaking engagements at venues all over the country.

The first time we stood on stage to talk about our adoption experience with a live audience, we were as nervous as you'd expect. Even though we'd already shown our lives to millions of people through *16 & Pregnant* and *Teen Mom*, it was a new experience to speak so honestly to a bunch of real-life faces turned toward us. But at the end of our first appearance, we were shocked by the applause we got. The crowd's reaction made it clear that our story really had meant something to these people. That was even more obvious when certain people from the audience approached us afterwards to thank us personally, ask for our advice, and tell us how much they had connected with our journey. And these weren't just teenagers, but people of all ages: adoptive parents, people who had been adopted, birth parents, and all kinds of people who had found something in our story to connect with. The first time someone told us we had inspired them to make an adoption plan, we knew this was something we had to keep pursuing. If one person in the audience is impacted positively by what we have to say, that's more than enough reason for us to keep sharing our story openly, honestly, and freely.

It was insane to look at each other and think, "Wow. Two kids from the trailer park are getting applause for being positive influences." It made us proud to realize how far we'd come, and it made us determined to make the most out of whatever opportunity we had to inspire people. We've worked so hard to get to the point where we feel like we're contributing something positive to the world in the way we live. Nothing could make us happier than to think that we've actually helped people with our experiences.

That was the spirit of writing this book. We're not life coaches or adoption gurus. We know we're still young, and we have plenty to learn. But we're in this privileged position of having a platform and an audience that's given us a chance to share whatever it is we have to offer. And what we have to offer is our story, our gratitude for anyone who's listened, and our best wishes for everyone out there who is struggling to do right in their lives and be the best people they can be.

Like we said in the very beginning, this book was written with one goal in mind: to inspire you. If we can spread a message of hope and positivity, that's what we want to do. For the kids growing up in trailer parks, unstable homes, or in the shadow of family problems and addiction. For the single moms working their butts off to take care of their kids no matter how hard they have to struggle. For the "bad kids" who can't seem to keep themselves out of trouble, and the parents and teachers who are trying to understand them. For the pregnant teens feeling lost and scared, and overwhelmed by their situations. For anyone who feels trapped in a cycle of dysfunction and wants to make something better of their lives. Whatever encouragement we can offer, we offer it from the bottom of our hearts.

We want to end this book the same way we always end our speaking engagements: With gratitude. No matter what you thought as you read this book, we know we would not be here if it wasn't for you and all of the other people who have given us a chance to tell our stories. We would not have the stability in our decision that we have now without the support so many strangers have given us. Not a day goes by when we don't give thanks for that support.

We would like to thank our parents, Carly, Brandon & Teresa, MTV, Jake and Nick at NBTV studios, and all the people who have supported us through the hardest times in our lives. You have no idea how crucial you all were in our healing process. Your love and dedication to our story humbles us everyday. We wouldn't be here without you. For all the people who have been inspired, uplifted and impacted by our story, this is for you because you are the reason we continue to share our story. You are the reason we make ourselves so vulnerable, and you are the reason that makes it all worth it... so thank you.

And finally, to the families affected by adoption, we hope we've done your experience justice. To our daughter Carly and to all of the other adopted children who may be reading this book: Never doubt how much love went into the choice your birth parents made. They did not give you up. They made a plan for you to have the best life they could possibly figure out how to offer you. And to all of those loving birth parents and adoptive parents, our hearts are full of understanding and admiration for the positive choices you have made for your children. Your struggles and sacrifices for the young lives who depend on you are worth everything in the world. From the bottom of our hearts, we wish you all the strength, positivity and love in the world.

With all our love,
Catelynn and Tyler